SWIMMING WITH THE FISHES

Fifty years of voluntary priests.

By Rev. Michael Johnson

Michael Johnson.

ISBN: 1482637030
ISBN-13:9781482637038

Introduction

I was born in Derbyshire in 1942, became a Christian whilst reading Chemistry at Birmingham University in 1961 and Ordained in 1971. I have worked as a self-supporting priest for over forty years before retirement at the age of seventy. All my priestly work involved developing ministry in my place of work in addition to a busy parish role. The story of my journey is written in the second chapter of 'Swimming With The Fishes'.

Married in 1965 to Barbara, two married children Rachel and Nicholas, and five grandchildren Nathan, Ben, Alice, Lizzie and Eleanor. I dedicate this book to these, my family.

The explanation of my book title is best understood by an early reading of these words which are to be found in a later chapter:

All priests are fishermen/women but we do our fishing in different waters, using different techniques. There is a communication between Non Stipendiary Ministers (NSMs) working within the M25, and one of its members Richard Spence makes an interesting point about 'fishing for men.' Simon Peter fished with nets and that's one way of capturing people and holding them until they reach land. Some use a lure to attract (an analogy might be the promise of eternal salvation if they get caught!). Yet others in the church make the equivalent of an attractive lobster pot with inviting things on offer inside, and wait for the fish to arrive. But the NSM takes to scuba diving, entering the fishes' own world in order to share their experience of God.

This where my title 'Swimming With the Fishes' comes from. In my ministry I have inhabited the environment of others and worked in their world.

MJ

CHAPTERS.

A brief preface to the theology which follows in subsequent chapters.

A look at St Paul's methodology and how it differs from today.

An account of the struggle to allow people in secular work to be ordained.

My recommendation of volunteer ministry as a high and ancient vocation.

Personal experience and the results from recent surveys.

Where do we go from here?

Chapter One

Foreword.

George MacLeod, of the Iona Community, said in 1958:

'I simply argue that the Cross be raised again at the centre of the market-place as well as on the steeple of the church. I am recovering the claim that Jesus was not crucified in a cathedral between two candles but on a cross between two thieves: on the town garbage heap; at a crossroad so cosmopolitan that they had to write his title in Hebrew and in Latin and in Greek; ... at the kind of place where cynics talk smut, and thieves curse, and soldiers gamble. Because that is where He died. And that is what He died about. And that is where churchmen should be.'

I wish I had written that – but it is what I would like to encourage. But how is it to be done? This book offers some thoughts about that question. The author, whose experience of priesthood is within Anglicanism, does not believe it can be done without radical change within the church, and that such a revolution will only come about after a rediscovery of particular aspects of New Testament practise. The ecclesiastical equivalent of rearranging the deckchairs on the Titanic will not do the trick. When in the Readers' Questions column of the church Times I read queries such as 'Is it ever permitted for a priest to say 'our sins' rather than 'your sins' when giving the absolution?', or 'Does church law allow a person to partake of Holy Communion more than once in the same day?', I have to restrain myself from writing back with the advice 'Get a life'! Another example, just read in this week's edition: 'My vicar has stopped saying 'Here endeth the lesson' at the end of his reading. Should I be exasperated?' No! - have you tried speaking to him?

I am not much exercised by questions about the length of lace on a cotta, or the most suitable width of a clerical collar. Because to Joe public who has no awareness of a relationship with God, such questions are quite irrelevant and very silly. Most priests have enough of a problem bridging the gulf between the pulpit and the pew, never mind tackling the abyss between the pew and the street outside. So what's to be done? This book will I hope provoke some discussion about what the church is, what it's for, and how it might be more closely linked with Christianity. I hope it will provoke both controversy and conversation.

I cannot trace the source of all my ideas, which have accumulated over many years. So I hope the reader will forgive if I am found to be repeating what others have said. I do not intend plagiarism, but if something I write appears to echo your own words, please take that as a compliment. My simplistic approach sees truth as truth whatever its origin, and truth bears repeating again and again because we follow a God who is Truth. Even when one person's truth is another person's heresy, at least the promotion of thought and discussion can't be bad. My first degree is in Science: there are still many who hold on to the nonsense that Christian faith and Science can never coexist. I know that to be false. Although my theological background and preference is relatively conservative and always Bible based, my pilgrimage has taught that both Science and faith share the experience of a ceaseless revision of hypothesis, quest, trial and experiment which leads to a deeper grasp of truth.

Part of what I write is a mini-autobiography which includes the experience of forty two years of ordained ministry in the workplace: I believe that where I am is partly explained by the route I have trodden thus far. It also serves to illustrate what the work of an NSM looks like in the church-world which shows little interest or understanding of it. In addition to developing mission in my places of work, I have at the same time been given main responsibility in eleven churches under a dozen bishops in three dioceses, often as the Village Priest (a title which ordinary folk found self-explanatory, unlike titles such as 'honorary assistant curate', etc). Over those years I have never taken fewer than sixty services annually.

I shall revisit the experience of the way the early church set up and enabled churches. I show how the movement to train and trust work-based ordained ministry has fared over the last century or so. I shall suggest where weaknesses in the present organisation of the C of E might be hindering rather than promoting God's work.

I write as an Anglican, and you may assume that my observations about 'the church' are chiefly based on the C of E. My hope would be that the C of E might rethink the default settings for the oversight of its parish churches and make it easier for the Holy Spirit to get a word in! For me, rightly or wrongly, freedom and grace always trumps canon law if there appears to be conflict, and the way I have sometimes done things has not always pleased some of the church hierarchy.

Chapter Two

My Personal Journey

It sometimes helps the reader to better understand (or excuse!) the opinions of the writer if he is made aware of the particular experiences which helped to shape his journey. The way travelled to some extent determines the path ahead. The Bible is full of the improbable journeys trodden by its heroes and villains; this is mine. I tell my story to illustrate that every Christian has a significant ministry which is often not planned, but follows naturally from commitment to a God who places us in situations where He is needed, if we allow. We are channels of God who communicates with His creation primarily through flesh and blood. We are missionaries whether trained or not, ordained or lay. It is often in looking back that we become aware of how often God has worked through us: His work, not ours. My belief is that all Christians should be able to say with St Paul:

'I have become all things to all people, that some may be saved.'

In my story there are so many occasions when things have happened to me, rather than having been pre-planned by me. There have been situations which do not

Michael Johnson

readily respond to simple logic or questions such as 'Why?' A good example of this, especially for the priest-worker is 'Why ordination, given that the situations you get involved in are likely to happen in the lives of lay Christians?' I cannot answer a question such as this except by suggesting that ordination is something that you are rather than something that you do, and that it happens to be God's decision how it all works. My point is that although many of the experiences I write about are likely to happen to any Christian, in fact they happened to me when ordained, trained and experienced, following expectations others laid on me because of the role they saw in me as a priest.

There is however a further factor in this, and that is how other people have expectations about a priest, just as they do about doctors or lawyers, and it is those expectations which often trigger a particular interaction. Whether dressed in priestly finery with a dog collar, wearing a simple cross, or just being open about being a Christian, people's expectations of us are changed quite profoundly. Ordained or lay, it's the 'leaven in the lump', the 'salt of the earth', the 'lamp on the lamp stand' effect which opens the channel through which God has His way. It might be useful to hold in one's mind the question 'Looking at Mike's ministry, how did priesthood change

10

things – was there more mission, or less, or was it just different?' What you will notice is that there was always some sort of ministry happening, never any period when I am redundant once I was a Christian, and this not of my choosing.

Birth to the End of the 1950's

In my immediate family nobody ever went to church – not even for times like Christmas and Easter – except for 'hatching, matching and dispatching'. Born into a Midlands mining community in the 1940's, religious rites of passage often took place in a Methodist Chapel because it was generally the case that the 'church people' came from a posher class than the chapel goers. However my paternal grandfather had been very active in the Methodist church, even getting his name on one of the foundation stones of the village Chapel and writing a book of theology which was never published. Mother was one of ten children and father one of seven, so the number of uncles and aunties (for they all married) was enormous, but churchgoing was not their habit.

Only my auntie Peggy (again on dad's side) who was a Methodist local preacher, told me later in life that she had always prayed for me. I think many of us have these quiet, anonymous 'angels' who channel the grace of

God without our ever knowing. But growing up I never had the urge to experience formal worship. Having said that, my father clearly had caught some of his father's faith which influenced the morality and tone of my upbringing. I think I would have been quite happy to go to church if only I had a friend to share it with .... and so it happened.

At Grammar School a multiplicity of extra-curricular fun was to be had in the many after-school societies: one of them was dancing lessons. So it was on December 18th 1959 that I went to Clay Cross Drill Hall (a post-war hangover) with most of the Sixth Form for an evening dance, and I needed a partner. Barbara – also in the Science Sixth – was that partner and we were destined to marry in 1965. She lived in a nearby village to mine, an easy trip on my motorbike. I soon found out that Barbara's fun time in her village revolved around a lively group of youngsters who had formed a youth organisation (oddly named 'The Squash') which they organised all by themselves.

In that village, in addition to the Parish church and a Pentecostal Gospel Hall (and never the twain shall meet) there were four Methodist churches – Zion Primitive, Wesleyan, Mount Tabor, and Bethel – and it was from these that the Squash was born. The young members, unlike their parents, thought it was foolish to have so many Methodist churches in one tiny village. So whilst it was unthinkable to go to the extremes they perceived in Anglicanism on the one hand or Pentecostalism on the other, they formed their own worship and fun group. They joked about going out one night and burning down all the chapels in the hope that only one would be built in their place! Of course, in such a situation all four would have been rebuilt! Today, one is a carpet warehouse, one an undertaker's Chapel of Rest, and so on.

I'd never met young Christians before. I marvelled that Christians could have so much fun together. The loud singing of Wesleyan hymns and choruses was great, as were the trips we organised for members of the Squash. We might go down to the local train station (pre-Beeching!) and ask that on a Bank Holiday Monday they put on an extra guards van for us – no problem. With back-packs and boots we'd go up to the Peak District, playing cricket in the Guards Van on the way up and back. We'd hire a bus and go to Cliff College (the Methodist Training College) to a 'Rally' to hear some evangelistic preaching. We'd travel to the Lake District for an outing together. All this was done without any adult intervention or control.

The First Half of the 1960's

It was great! All this fun and a girl friend too. I loved the Christian bit and happily called myself a Christian. In 1960 I went off to Birmingham University to read Chemistry, and Barbara was to follow to London University to read Biological Sciences. Younger readers could not imagine how different it was in those days to go to university. Nobody in my family had ever done such a thing (only about 3% went off to do a degree), and my parents' were so nonplussed that they prepared me by buying me a tailored raincoat, a rolled umbrella, a pair of leather gloves and a white silk scarf: they thought that's what posh people did. Barbara was offered a place at Oxford but turned it down because she could not cope with the accents she'd heard at the interview and was ashamed of her own - all unthinkable today.

At university fresher days new students wondered around being enticed to join this or that University Society. I'd enjoyed my experience of young Christians in The Squash, so I took a belt-and-braces approach and joined both the Methodist Society and the Christian Union. I was to discover that the each considered the other to be beyond the pale. Birmingham University Evangelical Christian Union (the name says it all) thought those in the 'Meth. Soc.' to be wishy-washy liberals: the latter responded by seeing BUECU members as Bible-bashing fanatics. No worry, I went to both, 'though I found that BUECU was more to my taste because there I had the Bible teaching which helped me to ground by Christian faith and introduced me to a love of theology. I began to devour Christian books – couldn't get enough of them. This certainly had an effect on my studies: I am ashamed to say that my devotion to learning about the faith meant that I was in my second year before I discovered where the University Library was! My science books were used, yes, but my Bible wore out and fell to pieces, most pages full of scribbled notes. I got highly involved in the BUECU Committee – at various times Mission Secretary, Treasurer, and so on, and went to all the weekends away where nationally known Christian speakers led our worship and teaching.

So towards the end of my first year at university my commitment had grown enormously, particularly my knowledge and understanding of Christian doctrine. Then just before term ended something extraordinary happened. Some will dismiss what follows as perhaps hallucination, or a dream, the fulfilment of a psychological wish. But to me it was the defining point of my Christian journey. At the same time I was Paul on the road to Damascus being told *'I am Jesus ..... you will be told what you must do'*. I was Peter at Caesaria

Philippi saying *'You are the Christ, the Son of the living God.'* I was Samuel saying *'Lord, here am I, send me.'* I was Moses at the burning bush, afraid to look at God. I was Jeremiah saying *'I do not know how to speak; I am only a child.'* So what happened?

In my lodgings in King's Heath, it was twenty minutes to midnight. I was in bed, the lights were out. Now the astonishing bit: I was suddenly aware that God was in the room. Overcome with emotion close to terror I kept my eyes closed so hard it hurt, and scrambled out of bed onto my knees. My heart was in overdrive and I was breathing heavily. In my head was a voice – not an audible one – which simply said 'I want you.' My response was to respond (again in my head) rather like John McEnroe at Wimbledon 'You cannot be serious!'. But his was followed by 'I'm really scared, I have no idea what you want of me, but I cannot resist. If you want me I'm yours.' Then, eyes still hard closed, I crawled back under the bed covers. Overcome by a feeling of warmth, joy and peace I quickly fell asleep and slept soundly. And that was it. I kept it to myself and life carried on as normal. Inside me I knew my world had changed, but had no idea what the outcome might be.

Before the end of term, at yet another session of Christian leaning I was challenged by the idea of tithing my income, giving a tenth to God as it were. It seemed a ridiculous idea. My parents could not afford a penny towards my university costs and my total grant was £180 a year to pay for everything. It was 1961 and my lodgings (with breakfast) were only £3 a week, but nevertheless my motorbike petrol was just over 5p a litre and I spent an average of almost £1 a week on food. So I had to borrow a bit from mum and dad, paying them back during the summer holidays. I earned money by working for the local council as a road labourer. It was good money at £13 a week, enabling me to repay any debts and pay mother the small rent she charged for living at home. So to give 10% of my grant to God seemed unlikely. After a while I took the plunge and told God he would have his 10%. The next morning I received a letter from the grant awarding body in Derbyshire, informing me that in the following year my grant was to be raised to £220. I have tithed ever since!

Summer came and went, and year two began in Birmingham. Again I plunged myself into my studies (a bit) and my Christian friends (a lot). My Chemistry Professor interviewed me to ask what 'additional studies' I was going to sign up for. We had to commit to a wider education than just our degree subject, and to a sport. I told him I would do Fencing and New Testament Greek.

An odd conversation took place: 'New Testament Greek? Nobody in my Chemistry Department has ever done that before.' 'So I'll be the first?' 'Well. I'm not fixing it up for you. You will need to go and sort it out yourself with the Professor of Theology, then let me know what happens.' 'OK'. And that is exactly what happened!

The business about tithing had started to teach me to trust God more. A theological question was nagging in my head. Just how much did I trust: just how much did God want? I decided that I had accepted Jesus as Saviour but not as Lord. I was very comfortable with the busy social life with great Christian friends and a sense of forgiveness, but was Jesus also my Master?

In those days the university Christian Unions were linked to the Inter Varsity Fellowship and had strong links with the Scripture Union. Both were to play a part in my activities. Members of the CU were expected every year to run a University Mission – a programme of activities designed to attract other students to events where they might hear and respond to the Christian message. We formed a strong relationship with a speaker called Roger Forster, who went on to found the Icthus movement. Roger was a great teacher of the faith and I loved to sit at his feet. One day I was sitting having a drink with him in the Student Union building when he said 'Mike, have you been baptised?' I said I had been told that as a baby I was christened in the village Methodist Chapel. He explained that it might help me if I had baptism as an adult believer, publicly telling my Christian story. Asking him how that might be organised, he half-jokingly said 'There's the fountain outside the window: we'll do it now if you like!'

Another arrangement was preferred which was almost as unusual. The next time I had a break from studies I would ride my motorbike down to North Kent to a Christian Fellowship group which Roger led, at a time when others were to be baptised too. This was done. The address was a private house: the baptism took place in their swimming pool in the garden, and Roger presented me with a very thick theological tome entitled 'Baptism'.

Members of the CU, 'though untrained and often young Christians, would be involved in invitations to speak at varied venues. Presumably those who gave the invitations were expecting a particular theological line from their speakers. I remember giving a talk at a mother and baby home. In the 1960's unmarried young mums were often hidden from view in a place where they had their baby and were encouraged to then have them adopted. I hate to think what I might have said to them. On another occasion I went to a small 'free church' I think they called themselves, in the Black Country. When I got there the meeting was in a converted public house, the etched windows still proclaiming 'Lounge Bar' or 'Public Bar.' An elder led me to the pulpit and said 'You'll notice on the pulpit shelf, minister, that there's some water and some oil, in case you feel the need for baptising or anointing somebody'. After my address one of the congregation stood up and said 'I think we should have a collection for this young man'. He passed around his flat cap, then brought it to me with the suggestion that I could do what I liked with it!

Holidays from university began to be filled with Christian service rather than road building. The Scripture Union in London always had voluntary work available there, and after all that's where Barbara lived at university. One summer was spent going to London railway stations and actively looking for the arrival of foreign students prior to the university term. The technique was to home-in on anyone who looked foreign and was carrying bags. I would ask if they were coming into England for the first time to study, and if so I could offer practical help. This might involve negotiating the Tube network with them to find their overnight stay, generally introducing them to their new country. Younger readers will not be aware how different was the situation then. I remember one African student telling me after his overnight stay that he had been very cold. On questioning I found that he had no idea how to use an English bed, and had slept on top of the covers. Once the arrivals had been helped as much as was reasonable, the pay off was to offer them a little booklet from the Scripture Union, telling the Christian message.

Holidays were very precious to Barbara and I, so we looked for a joint activity during the long summer break so that we could be together. We decided to work for one of the Scripture Union Missions on the banks of Lake Windermere in Cumbria. Within two years we found ourselves leading the team of about thirty young people for several weeks each summer. Living was very basic, in an empty school where (reasons below) we had seven gas ovens installed before our arrival. Sub-teams looked after different sections of the mission – children's activities, youth, families. I led the youth team in a converted hay loft which we called the Saints and Sinners Club. In the day we wandered amongst the tourists giving invitations to the Club. For teenagers the day died about tea-time, so we offered a late opportunity in our coffee bar for friendship and fun. Fun was different then. We opened in the evening and closed when the last person left after midnight wearing a club badge. The team members fell asleep amongst the crisp packets and fag ash.

As well as friendship, drinks and crisps we always had people with guitars. People sat around singing from a song book which we produced (a mixture of folk and Christian songs) and the team told their stories. This simple device connected with many young people who were wandering through the district, discovering themselves and life itself. It is interesting to note that many had tales to tell, to which nobody had ever listened. There was a young girl who brought her own guitar and told us her Christian story in a most engaging way. She told me she had been a covert Christian for thirteen years and had never had the opportunity to tell anyone, but now she could 'come out' as it were about her faith.

There was a young man from Liverpool who I asked to come with me on a rowing boat to one of the islands to cut wood for a BBQ. He told me (with an axe in his hand!) that he was just out of prison for shooting two people. Most of his life had been in some sort of institution. That week he became a Christian and promised to come back the following year. Keeping his promise he later told me how he had gone to apologise to his victims, even to the extent of buying five shirts and returning them to the shop from where he stole them. Every year there were such stories.

Fridays was family BBQ day. Early in the morning we bought seventy frozen chickens. Whilst solid, these were quartered with an axe and hammer we kept for the purpose. Once thawed they were boiled in huge cauldrons, then made to look good by browning them in our seven ovens. Finally they were wrapped in foil and packed in straw in tea chests to take to the BBQ. Enough people came to eat the lot. Visitors were subjected (apparently happily – they knew what they were signing up for) to singing and listening to the Christian message.

For the talk we had a huge marquee which needed guarding when not in use, to prevent vandalism or use as a free sleeping area. So one of the team would go each night and guard it. It was spooky. One night there had been a knife fight outside the marquee. The next day was my turn to sleep there and I was terrified at the prospect. As I got into my sleeping bag, very lonely, I prayed 'Lord, keep me safe tonight.' There was a noise at the entrance as the flap began to move. A huge dog came in, lay at the entrance and we both slept like babies.

All this gives a flavour of the adventures we had as young Christians willing to trust God for our lives. They were good times, but they were of their time – not appropriate today perhaps. My improbable Christian journey had got off to a busy start.

The Second Half of the 1960's.

After graduating I took a Post Graduate Certificate in Education and began to look for a job teaching Chemistry in London. Barbara was doing post graduate research and so such a job would give us an opportunity to get to know each other better before our planned wedding in the following year, 1965. But how was I to know what Chemistry teaching jobs were available in London?

Barbara, like many students, went to Westminster Chapel to hear the oratory of Dr Martyn Lloyd Jones, whose expository sermons were legendary: I remember him speaking for forty minutes on the word 'therefore'. One Sunday, coming down the steps she bumped into our old Religious Education teacher from our Derbyshire Grammar School. Knowing we were together, he asked Barbara how I was getting on. She explained that I had just got my post-graduate qualification and was looking for a Chemistry post in London. He responded by saying that in his school (a two thousand Comprehensive in South London) they had just interviewed for such a job but found no suitable candidate – I should write to the headteacher. This I did, receiving an invitation to go for an interview. My trusty BSA 600 and side-car made their way to London and I got the job, starting September

1964. I stayed in lodgings until we married on Easter Saturday 1965.

I enjoyed teaching a great deal, staying at that school for ten years and holding six posts. One of these was a sinecure: I was made Head of Annex, but we did not have an annex. The Head wanted me as Head of Sixth Form but the job was not available for a term, so he invented a post to keep me there! But I get ahead of myself.

Following our wedding, the purchase of a car for £35 and a week of honeymooning in a mobile home on Selsey Bill, we moved to a top floor flat in Blackheath Village. Our joint bank account held £50 after the wedding so, knowing we had to have somewhere to sleep, somewhere to keep clothes neat and somewhere to eat, we had bought a bed-settee, a wardrobe and a table with chairs. The flat was almost uninhabitable – gas lighting and no hot water – but over time I rewired the place, put in a gas water heater, built a mock fireplace with a gas fire, and so on. Indeed when we left, the ninety year old landlady who had been charging us £3 a week paid me £70 for the improvements we had made.

But back to the start, and another of those extraordinary coincidences which Christians call acts of

God. When we returned from our honeymoon, at ten o'clock in the evening, we had a caller to our new flat. The old lady was a stranger to us. She said that she worshipped at a nearby church. She had been told (How? Who? Why?) that two young Christians had just moved in. The church needed help and she wondered if we would be willing to go to her church and see if we fitted in to the slot they needed. To this day we have no idea how she knew we were there. The church was St James, Kidbrooke, a place with a lively, talented congregation and the sort of vicar we could work with: that means he was willing to bend rules for the sake of the gospel, and to think outside the box. With another young lady of our age we started a youth group, of which more later.

At school I found it natural to get stuck in to some Christian work, starting a Bible group which met at lunchtimes. Later (after ordination) I also ran lunchtime Holy Communion, and was often asked to help pastorally with both staff, students and parents – just because I was a priest. The headteacher had changed, the new man being a Methodist local preacher. There was a hall big enough to take a whole school assemblies of two thousand pupils and one hundred staff. I was placed on the assembly rota. Trying to bring a semblance if life into assembly I tended to work hard to connect with the students, even at the experience of upsetting the headteacher. Once I did this big time.

The headmaster asked me to take a harvest assembly. At that time the makers of Guinness had a slogan 'there's a whole world in a bottle of Guinness.' I thought I could use that. At the start of my talk I walked to sit at the grand piano on stage (I could not play it), pretended to begin but stopped short of the keyboard. I stood up, propped open the large lid, reached inside and pulled from the innards a bottle of Guinness with the words 'there's a whole world in a bottle of Guinness'. I had their attention. Using my Chemical knowledge I explained how the glass used sand washed by the sea, the cork inside the lid from African trees, the yeast ... the hops ... the malt ... the label and its ink .. and so on. Many people from many countries had worked together to produce this product: there was indeed a world of people cooperating and working together to harvest the goodness of nature. I was quite pleased. The head carpeted me for bringing alcohol into school!

I was to cross him a lot, and I tell this tale to illustrate how opportunities (perhaps truth, justice) crop up in Christian life. He was very dictatorial with staff and students alike. If you have seen the film 'Clockwise' starring John Cleese as the headteacher, it begins with the head looking through binoculars, spying on pupils arriving on the school premises from the comfort of his office. The film was based on 'my' headteacher. I was in his study when he told me he was having that window put in so he could spy on pupils. Outside his door he had a microphone installed so he could listen to the conversation of wayward students sent to him, before he let them in. Every classroom had a tannoy and a microphone – a lesson might be interrupted by 'Mr. X, please keep your class quiet.' As a class tutor I was required to check each of my tutor group weekly for correct uniform as specified on the official list. I refused to check if the girls were wearing green knickers. He caned pupils seen smoking in Lewisham on Saturdays! I spent time with his deputy when he had reduced her to tears. The real crunch came when I was Head of Sixth Form.

The dictator Idi Amin threw the Asians out of Uganda. Having English passports, many came to London, dozens to my school. They worked hard and achieved very well. The headteacher had a school rule that no boy could grow their hair longer than their shirt collar. This, despite their religion, included the Sikh Asian community. One of my academic stars had achieved eight O level examinations at top grades and was placed to get four good A levels. Several universities offered Anup a place. Before the A level examinations there was a long period when students stayed at home to revise. When Anup turned up for his first written examination paper his hair had grown. The head called me to his office – one of my pupils had hair longer than regulation and I had allowed him to sit an examination. He said he would write to every university on Anup's list and tell them to cancel his application because of his disobedience. I said that if he did that, I would resign.

He decided that he could not allow my resignation: his solution was to allow Anup to sit his examinations in a room by himself and go to his chosen university. As for me, there was a new school being built in London, for which he would write me an excellent reference if I applied to become its first headteacher - if I would stay. This approached bribery, and anyway I wasn't ready for headship. The term ended, Anup got his chosen university and I got a job at another school – two thousand, two hundred Comprehensive this time in North Kent. I loved large Comprehensives and before the end of my career I had close contact with ten thousand teenagers – what a privilege.

Over that same period in which I was busy establishing my teaching role. We were very busy in the parish church which had so mysteriously asked for help. Our work with youth focussed that part of our mission. It was a lively church – worshippers at the main Holy Communion about a hundred – with a sister church too. There was a rebel rector and a crazy curate in addition to two or three priests emerging from the recently established Southwark Ordination Course. The main church had its rectory within its land, a bungalow for the caretaker and his wife and a very large Hall.

With a small team we organised a club for the unclubables. In the 1960's it seemed that almost everyone of a certain age was part of a rock group, playing guitar, keyboard, drums, ... So we began the 'Friday Beat Club' which met each week in the church hall. Each week we hired one of several amateur groups to play extraordinarily loud, for want of a better term, music, and people paid a small sum to cavort around the floor for an hour or two. Simple refreshment was on sale. The popularity far exceeded our expectations and soon we had three hundred and seventy paid-up members of the Beat Club. In our naivety we could hardly predict what the outcome of this might be, but from our point of view it was to be the springboard for introducing young people to the Christian message.

First the good news: all sorts of positive things came

out of the Beat Club. With the help of a member of the congregation who was a TV producer, we put on productions in church. Perhaps the most ambitious and memorable was a rock opera called 'A Man Dies'. The Passion story was told with a large cast of club members, music, back-projection of dramatic imagery on a huge muslin screen – it was great. The churchwardens questioned the wisdom of having a BSA 650 twin motorbike in church, revving up and driving down the aisle, but it was part of the sung message: ('Just sixteen, got me a 'bike: £5 deposit, pay the rest when you like'.) But the drama produced tears when one of the club members, stripped to the waist, dragged a huge wooden cross down the aisle, his shoulder bleeding. That performance taught that young man a little of what true sacrifice looked like and felt like, and others knew it too.

Other productions were perhaps not as good. What comes to mind was a Christmas Nativity we wrote to support the homeless charity 'Shelter'. An unfortunate choice of club member to play Mary, combined with insufficient rehearsal for the baby Jesus doll, resulted in Mary looking out of her tent (well, it was about homelessness) and asking the large congregation 'Where's me bleedin' baby?' Similarly the members of the Beat Club did not always behave the way one had hoped on church property: more than once the incumbent would pop into the Club to tell us 'They are fornicating around the dustbins again!'

But the point was this: we built relationships with people who had no real likelihood of going into a church or meeting the Christian message. Members were visited in prison, others came to our flat to voice their problems. One gang leader told Barbara and I, how as a boy he was strapped to the end of a bed when his father needed to go out drinking, and was frequently beaten viciously. We were on a steep learning curve about why some people behaved the way they did.

We did our best to channel the aggression of street gang members. One thing we did was quite bizarre but a whole load of fun. Once a year we had a 'piano bashing contest'. For some reason, an appeal to the community for old pianos they wanted to get rid of, always resulted in donations of upright pianos. Lots of people had a worn-out instrument nobody played. So on the day of the contest different teams of Club members were given a piano and a sledge hammer. The rules were simple: get the entire piano, cast iron frame and all, through the hole of a lavatory seat hanging from a tree in the shortest time!

The way club members behaved was the reason why the Friday Beat Club met an unfortunate end, 'though happily this was after a significant time. From Greenwich we attracted two rival street gangs. There were petty crimes in the club – perhaps stealing someone's leather coat – and an increasing number of fights. The tension would rise until someone took a plate from the kitchen, smashed it into shards and threw these to fellow gang members as weapons. Clearly we had to involve the police by asking for help. They were initially happy about this: we were keeping a lot of trouble off the street, and some members were having their lives turned round. Sometimes a couple of young police would come incognito to mingle, in case of trouble or because there had been a flare-up the previous week.

However gang members were always able to recognise a policeman out of uniform. There were some bad incidents, such as when an unhinged club member leapt onto the stage, put his foot through a drum and bit a chunk off the drummer's ear – for fun! The crunch came when one policeman had his sheepskin coat stolen. His colleagues picked up a few young club members who were not responsible, hoping to get some intelligence from them. They took minors to the police station, kept them without telling parents, and so on - in short the police broke their own rules. Our club leaders told the police they would not act as witnesses in court without pointing out how the innocent youngsters had been treated unlawfully. We could not afford to lose the trust of our club members. We had an anonymous call from the police which said that because of our decision not to support them, the next time there was a fight and we asked for help, they would not be coming. We could not run the club without the back-up of the police as a safeguard, so we had to close.

It's interesting how God's plans for oneself become plain, and in retrospect I realised He had something else in mind for me around this time, 1967. I had only been teaching three years, our marriage was established (with the thought of starting a family) and we had begun to think about buying our own house in South London. Barbara had finished her post graduate research and was involved in lecturing in the Biological Sciences. In today's terms, salaries were tiny, but then so were house prices. When I started teaching, non graduates earned £730 annually but I started on £800. Now we both earned more than that, and mortgages were offering up to two and a half times one's joint income. So we had enough to qualify for a loan on a four year old terraced house priced at £3,700. In that house by 1970 we had two children –

literally in the house because at that time the London Borough of Lewisham encouraged DIY (if necessary) home births! Indeed for the first birth, our daughter, the midwife was still in training and there was no doctor.

Before that happened I had been bothered by one of those ideas which rattles around in one's head and will not let go however preposterous it seems – I should get ordained. I loved teaching, was good at it and definitely had cut out a ministry for myself there. If I could train on the Southwark Ordination Course, as some friends at church had done, I could carry on teaching. On the other hand the idea seemed daft – officially I was a card-carrying Methodist working in an Anglican church, and to be frank I didn't really like the C of E as much as I liked Methodist worship.

The idea would not go away. One day I telephoned my vicar 'Michael, there's something I need to see you about. When might I come for a chat?' The following Thursday evening I knocked on the rectory door. He opened it and said 'Mike. I don't know what you want to talk to me about, but when you've finished will you stay a bit longer? I think you should get ordained.' God does like a laugh doesn't he?

As a further illustration that rules can be bent when

God's at work, I relate a very odd telephone call I had from Bishop Mervyn Stockwood, which went something like this. 'Mike, I understand that you have been selected for ordination and have gained a place on the Southwark Ordination Course.' 'Yes Bishop'. 'But at the end of it I will not be able to ordain you because you have never been Confirmed.' 'That's right Bishop'. 'I understand that you are occasionally preaching and administering Holy Communion without my permission.' 'Yes Bishop'. 'I cannot come to your church to confirm you because it will upset a number of the congregation once they realise you are not an Anglican.' 'So what shall we do Bishop?' 'Come to the Cathedral next week and be confirmed along with other candidates; nobody need know about it!' And so I became a reluctant member of the C of E. I guess that having been christened as a baby, baptised as an adult, formally entered into the membership of the Methodist church and now confirmed, I had jumped through more hoops than most!

Three very difficult years followed which came near to breaking our marriage. Ordination training on top of a very busy career at the same time that we were having two children, moving house and my wife losing some of her identity because of giving up lecturing for a while – these are major stress events. But there was something else which was going to change our lives at the same time. The Greater London Council was planning a huge housing development near where our parish church was. Thousands of people would move out from inner London to live in what was presented as a higher class, high specification scheme – a description not even close to the eventual reality of a concrete jungle of tower blocks and walkways which has since been bulldozed. At the planning stage the church had to be involved. In discussion with my vicar we suggested that after my training was complete I could lead the church work in the new community. We went to County Hall to meet in discussion with the planners, to tell them our vision.

We explained perhaps to their relief that we were not asking for a traditional church building. Although in the late 1960's the idea of planting alternative expressions of church had not become fashionable, we were well into that concept. This was our plan: we would like a shop unit. On the plans this was a concrete tunnel ten feet high and twenty feet wide, forty feet long, with living accommodation above. I would plan its interior which would be flexible – for instance a café/meeting place staffed by church workers, converted into a worship area at weekends. This was agreed but there was a problem. The estate would be separated by a main road. The first phase (on one side) consisted of housing only. The other phase of shops, a pub, hall, etc. would follow afterwards, so we could not have a shop unit for at least a year after the first phase.

We should have realised then that the GLC planners had little idea of what a community needed to work properly. So we had to suggest a compromise. If they could offer us a four bedroomed council house with the first wave of tenants, we would operate that as the church until the shop unit was built. It had an extra bedroom which could be my study, a larger main room for worship of a dozen or so adults, and a large kitchen for the Sunday School. The church lent me a portable ancient font which I could carry round to baptise babies in their own gardens. Yes, I know what you are thinking – you were very naïve and it won't work. In some ways you are right.

My ordination was due at Michaelmas 1971, but the GLC said the council house would be ready in 1970. They gave us a date for moving in. We put our house on the market at £500 more than we paid for it and at a financially disastrous time, because unknown to us house prices rocketed immediately afterwards and had we sold it a year later (see below) it would have fetched £6,000. A buyer came along and we legally signed the house away, ready to move when the GLC moving date was promised.

Immediately a letter arrived saying we could not have the council property until three months after the expected date: they had found a structural fault in a similar block and all had to be checked. We were potentially homeless, with a baby and a toddler. Bishop Mervyn stepped in and offered us an empty vicarage a few miles away which would be OK until the new incumbent arrived in three months. As soon as we moved there the GLC contacted again – the council house would not be available for at least six months. I created a fuss and the GLC offered us a house located in our home parish as a temporary solution: it was to be bulldozed for a road extension. So in fact we lived for twelve months out of boxes, never unpacking everything, and moved onto the Ferrier Estate a year later than expected. We had been seriously damaged by the experience. Mervyn Stockwood perhaps recognised that we had had a rough time and knowing our financial situation he kindly gave us £70 to buy new curtains for the Council house.

In the first fortnight just a handful were moved in, including next door to us a GP. These two professionals (potential priest and a doctor) were expected to be there to serve the new community as it arrived. But I had a busy job, the GP was full of problems and whisky, and the residents who moved in often had major problems. There were hundreds of dwellings, but no shop, pub, meeting place, bus service, school – nothing to support community. It was very difficult for Barbara: a toddler and a baby, bothered by visitors demanding my time, isolated without even a home of her own because it was full of 'church' on Sundays. I suppose that was good – people did come, did want babies baptised. A few were wonderful Christians who are still friends over forty years later. For my part I had a job I loved, kept being promoted, and enjoyed the collegiate life of the Southwark Ordination Course with its monthly residential weekends. Barbara had almost nothing.

There was plenty to do all right. People came to our house church. We got a bus service to Lewisham. Barbara started a very successful play group, taking people by minibus up to our old church hall. But when she asked the GLC for an on-site facility, they offered a corridor on a third floor with swing doors at both ends! They were hopeless at almost every level, their thoughtless planning even resulting in the tower blocks having lifts so small that when people died, the coffin had to travel vertically. The other half of the estate with school, shops, etc. was not available in the first year.

Social problems were huge: this was the estate where the heavily bitten body of little Maria Colwell was found, murdered by her dad in a case which shocked the nation and opened people's consciousness about child abuse. As the news broke, Spike Milligan was in a taxi 'to some pointless place'. On a scrap of paper he wrote this wonderfully tender tribute:

Goodnight Maria. They have just changed you from one darkness to another. You left behind the eternal promise of light, of seedlings left in cruel adult frosts. When Spring comes, how many will miss your flower? If you had grown in my garden we would have won prizes together. Goodbye Maria. Your gardeners are still alive.

One of my regular 'congregation' was totally bed-ridden on the tenth floor of a tower block. She had an important position in a London Company until one day, whilst commuting to work, the Tube electricians went on strike and switched off the escalators. She tumbled down and many landed on top of her. The damage to her lungs was permanent – for many years she depended on bottled oxygen and was barely able to walk a step. She had her very low points whilst living in the GLC estate.

One evening she told me that during the day she had tried to commit suicide by getting out of the window, but was physically unable to climb out. So this night she would overdose on Warfarin which she had hidden in so many places that however much I searched, I would not find it all. Giving me the key, and saying that as a Christian she had no fear of death, she asked me to come in at 6.30 the next morning before I went to school and to make the required arrangements. When I went in next morning she had changed her mind. In fact Barbara and I were with her when she was near to death a few years later, by which time she had secured a bungalow in the market town of Faversham, close to where we then lived. Telling us she was already walking the path to her end, comfortable in her faith, she died that night and I was able to take her funeral at Davington.

It was clear that work on the estate was going to destroy our marriage, kill us, or both! It had already got rid of our life savings. I was fortunate at that time to have a brilliant Suffragan Bishop in David Sheppard before he became Bishop of Liverpool. When I told him of our position after about 18 months on the estate, giving him six months notice of our leaving, he was totally sympathetic. When we left the work had grown so much that we were replaced by one full-time priest and a half-timer. The shop unit was completed after we left and was christened the Phoenix Centre. We left London behind and moved to North Kent. Soon I left my Comprehensive School and found a larger one in our new town.

1973 to 1989.

With help from parents we put down the deposit on another house. Life was a good deal more ordered and this helped old wounds to heal. Barbara returned to lecturing because we were able to house an au pair to help with the children. It was a good move. What's more when Gun (from Sweden) married her English beau, she was replaced by her twin sister Siv who also settled down eventually with an English husband. The town where we lived had a very High Anglican church which wasn't my cup of tea because without an Anglican upbringing I had very little idea of what was going on, and hated the intoning of readings, psalms and prayers.

However nearby was a benefice of three churches in the Darent Valley overseen by an incumbent who welcomed me warmly. He too had been in secular work before ordination (as a stipendiary) and I think his understanding of the pressures in my work life helped. He had been in advertising until as he used to say, he had finally found something supremely worth advertising! Licensed to those three churches by my new Bishop of Rochester, one particular parish Farningham, was as it were given to me. For many years I was able to contribute very fully to parish life, especially at weekends. I also took services at Eynsford and Lullingstone Castle, loving the warmth and fellowship of those parishioners.

Being in senior management at school (Head of Science and Mathematics Faculty with 28 staff of my own) I had opportunities for new adventures there. In a school of that size there were loads of Christian pupils and staff, enough to organise Christian groups. They all knew of course that I was ordained, and this meant they sought me out for specific help. I married staff and ex-pupils, took funerals, and so on. Over the road was the C of E Primary school where our children went; there I was invited to take regular Holy Communion services as required. When our two offspring reached eleven years old, they crossed the road to their dad's school and both did extremely well academically and socially there. I was usually able to relieve them of the embarrassment of being their teacher because I wrote the timetable. In pre-computer days this task took six weeks, ensuring that one hundred staff got the correct students in one hundred rooms on two sites over a two week timetable. I was later to realise that running a small parish was no match for that sort of organisation!

It is interesting how others have expectations of someone simply on the grounds that you are ordained. Quite often it is my experience that NSMs will be given additional roles in the workplace because it is expected that they are equipped to do an honourable job. To some extent such expectations define the shape of your role and you are thrust into new situations not of your own making. An example, unusual enough to make the point. At school we had a new Humanities teacher who was absolutely hopeless with the children. They ran rings round him, and he seemed unable to cope even though he was given a great deal of support. He decided to air his frustrations in the national press, blaming his troubles on the headteacher in particular and Comprehensive schools in general. Governors and even the parish Council considered that it was not the school at fault. The teacher's rantings grew until TV picked it up. At that time the Irish television presenter Eamonn Andrews of 'This Is Your Life' fame had a daily evening programme, at 6.00 pm I think.

I was in my first term at my new school. The headteacher called me in before school began. He told me that the TV Company had just 'phoned to say that the troublesome teacher was being interviewed on the show that evening, and they had offered the school the opportunity to be part of the discussion. My headteacher wanted me to go because he thought that if my name on screen were prefaced by 'The Rev.' it would carry greater weight! He gave me the day off to prepare and I went on live after The Supremes had done their singing. In the event the teacher made a very poor showing whilst I had gone very well prepared to win the argument. Afterwards I was told there was a car waiting outside to take me to the station (useful because the fee of £11 did not go far!) It was time for me to make a fool of myself. Outside the studio I approached the uniformed chauffeur in front of a limousine to be told 'No sir: this is for the Supremes. Yours is the black cab.'

In my new job, new home, new parishes, Barbara able at last to exercise again her academic talents and use them well, children at school with shared care from an au pair they loved, life gained a new balance and stability. It was to be about seventeen years before we left that situation (although of course our jobs changed, we moved house, the children grew up, and so on.) For the first (but not last) time I was to discover that God would use me very fully both in a work situation and whilst working in a multi-parish benefice where I had overall responsibility for at least one parish. In a nutshell, yes, it worked very well. I established that some of my

Christian role at school was to stand up for the underdog – attending tribunals, championing the rights of oppressed or at-risk teenagers whose lives were made hell by inadequate parenting or abuse. I felt that my work as a priest gave me a wider 'parish' than could have been achieved if confined to a parochial system.

That is not to say that the voluntary priesthood suggests a pattern for the whole of the C of E, because there is no way I could have held down senior management posts in large schools and at the same time been able to run a busy city/urban church. Without pretending to be some sort of superhero, I was to discover for the rest of my ministry that in terms of organisation and time, if one is competent at managing up to two thousand pupils, one hundred staff and a seven figure budget, it is possible at the same time to run a rural parish. The parish work is not as it was a couple of generations ago: the community does not expect their parish priest to go 'cold calling' throughout the village, and so on. They need the priest there for serious illness, for baptisms, marriages, funerals, regular Sunday worship and the like. But in a typical rural community it would be unusual in my experience to have as many as twenty Occasional Offices each year.

The rural situation can be much more readily

predicted and controlled. Contrast this to when I was on a Crematorium rota in a busy London Borough where I could be called to deal at short notice with the death in a family I had never met, and shoot off to earn my fee of thirty bob (£1.50) taking the Crematorium service! That's not what the life of a 'proper' priest should ever be but it is worth mentioning that even in such barren landscape God often used the situation. However I can appreciate that even in a very busy parish a group of ordained worker priests could usefully share tasks like that and still have time to make more meaningful relationships within their formal role.

Of course I will not pretend that 'having two jobs' is ever an easy option but it was what God had wanted me to do. It was very hard, but we were sustained in it. Over four decades (until retirement) there was only one occasion when I had three Sundays in succession free from church responsibility. OK, that was my choice, my fault if you like. But there is another side to that which needs to be considered by the hierarchy of the church. First, an analogy. In one school a long-service headteacher left. After the farewell, as is the nature of school staff rooms, colleagues were discussing his legacy. A head of department said to me: 'I won't forgive him for never coming into my classroom throughout my time here, never popping his nose round the door and saying 'How's it going?"

The work of a volunteer minister can mirror that loneliness and lack of support – not from one's local benefice colleagues, but from the diocesan hierarchy to whom one feels invisible. A stipendiary priest would have much more pastoral oversight than I was ever given, perhaps offered a sabbatical after a decade or two. We are often doing key outreach work about which the bishop often seemed to have no knowledge and in which he took no interest.

For me, I was a priest at work, and I was a priest in the parish. Teaching Chemistry, being in senior management, opened so many doors to living out the Christian good news. It's all about human relationships. Over my teaching career I had personal contact with about ten thousand teenagers. What a privilege, what a responsibility! We all remember our teachers (for one reason or another!) The most touching card I ever received was from a Sixth Form pupil who had been in my class. Before they left for University this farewell card said 'Thank you so much for teaching me more than just Chemistry.' That young lady had grown through my classes, got to trust me, shared her faith, been part of a Christian study group I ran in this secular school, etc.

Looking back to those relationships with young Christians, I sometimes wonder if I should always have formally contacted the parish priest to which those young people 'belonged'. I don't think this is cut and dried. It is inevitable that a volunteer priest will work outside their own parish boundary and often outside their own diocesan area. Do we need to set up a system to formalise that reality? For some of the pupils, school was their parish for a time, the school Christian group meeting one lunchtime was their church.

For most of the pupils I was the only priest they had ever met. In connection with every school in which I taught, there were for years telephone calls which began with conversations such as: 'Hello Mr Johnson. You might not remember me, but my name is XY and I was one of your pupils. You are the only vicar I know and I wonder if you can help me ....' Sometimes it was because of trouble, sometimes it was happy ('will you marry me to my partner: will you baptise my baby', etc). But the key phrase was 'you are the only vicar I know'. They had decided they needed a vicar and had no idea how to access their allotted one, 'though of course in many cases I was happy to contact their parish priest. With the cooperation, indeed blessing of many parish priests, I was able to personally serve the need of that ex-pupil by arranging a service in their own parish and ministering there, further developing an established relationship.

Sometimes the need of a pupil was not priest-oriented in that way, but I was in the right place at the right time to give help, that help being largely directed by my faith. Let me give an example. When I as First Deputy Headteacher in another London school, a fourteen year old girl entered my office. I saw a lot of her – many staff found her very difficult, insolent, unruly, and she was frequently 'sent' to me. We had developed a relationship in which she knew I would back up my staff whilst at the same time be very fair to her, giving her a sanctuary to settle herself down until she could cope. This time she was quiet and said she had asked her class teacher to allow her to come to me for an important talk. It is likely that her subject teacher was glad to be rid of her for half an hour. She was clearly troubled as she told me that she wanted to discuss something which was the background cause of all her poor behaviour – could she please share something private with me.

I guessed what she might be ready to tell me. I said to her that I would be very happy to listen to her, to help her, but she should be aware that there are some things which I could not legally keep to myself. On that basis, did she still want to tell me her story? She agreed. My intuition was correct. The girl had been sexually abused by her father from an early age, with the knowledge of her mother. She could not stand it any longer and wanted out, whatever the consequences.

We had a long chat. I involved the police and social services. That girl never went home again. Her clothes, toys and other belongings were collected by the authorities and taken to her in a secret safe place. I saw her at case meetings, but otherwise she had effectively vanished from the area to start afresh and put herself back together with professional help. I was there when she needed me, trusted enough from our past relationship, and from my point of view I was glad to offer what I feel is a priestly ministry, however unusual. Not many priests ever get that sort of privilege.

I was happy to be busy in a traditional parish situation where the fact that I was paid or not was of no importance to the congregation and village. On most occasions I was serving a parish which could not afford a priest 'of their own' and they had lost their vicarage with its occupant many years ago. Indeed, in my current four-parish benefice there are at least six homes labelled 'rectory' or 'vicarage', but five of those have been sold by the diocese to private buyers, and homes which were used for curates in training are also lost.

Lifelong friends were made. My two ministries overlapped – my children and their school friends (from my school) were sharing lives with me in home, school and parish. At my retirement party a significant number of ex-pupils were there with their spouses and children. Somehow the separations between church life, home life and work life seemed to have been bridged by this sort of role multitasking. I also found it most helpful to the benefice to keep the ship afloat during interregna and certainly the parishioners voiced their warm gratitude for that on three occasions.

During my time in North Kent serving parishes in the Darent Valley, I took another post in the London Borough of Greenwich for about nine years. This was my first experience of a Church of England Comprehensive School. It was a wonderful experience (despite many 'tough' pupils) to work in a Christian School. The Governors had decided that all senior management must be practising Christians and that all appointed staff should be prepared to support the Christian ethic. The mutual commitment was welcome and evident, the Christian service given by staff overt. Crises were shared and Christian support available.

This example will illustrate how that worked out. One year I began in September a GCSE Chemistry class of fourteen year olds, of which two were to die that year. One girl died of breast cancer: one boy of bone cancer. The girl was from an African Christian background and that helped them enormously. The boy was not a Christian and came from Hong Kong. He went from healthy to dead in six weeks. Both staff and pupils readily visited him in hospital. There he asked for baptism and it was given. His memorial service, with all the senior school present, took place in my old church, St James in Kidbrooke, from where I had been ordained. His coffin stood in the aisle. At the end of the service each class began in turn to file out of church. One boy turned round and walked back to the coffin. Nobody stopped him. When he reached his old friend he tapped the top of the box and said 'See you later Chu', then quietly left. It was a magic moment.

After about eight years in that school I had another of those odd experiences that Christians sometimes experience – the strong conviction that, however happy or successful one is, it is time to move on. I could not shake it off. Wise or foolish, I made a pact with God which went something like this. One of my responsibilities was to write the school timetable. In the Senior Management team we had started to think about fundamental reorganisation which would have to be reflected in the next year's timetable if it were to be realised. This is a process which unfortunately is much more difficult in a church.

We pretended we could start from scratch and ask the question 'If we had a clean slate, how would we structure this school?' The idea is to write a 'shadow structure' towards which, as staff came and went, the school would be steered over a few years until the preferred structure were reached. Part of our decision, given that I gave a year's notice, was to split my job into two. One person would be in charge of the upper school, one the lower school, under a Principal. Whatever the outcome I would write myself out of next years timetable. That was my way of saying to God 'OK, over to you: I won't have a job here in twelve months'.

What was I to do? I wanted to be in charge of whatever work I had. So I decided to apply for headships back in Kent. Was it foolish? - I made conditions! It had to be the headship of a mixed Comprehensive school. Readers might not be aware that unlike most of the country, Kent has very few of those – it still has the equivalent of the 11-plus, and Grammar schools. Nevertheless over the next twelve months four such posts came available. I applied for all four. I got an interview for all four. At the end of every deliberation I was told by the senior inspector that I had come second – please keep trying! Again I asked the question: what was I to do? I had burned my boats. What was God saying?

With the support of my wife but with very little forward planning we thought that our lives were stable enough to take some chances. One child married, one at University and an empty nest. I might change profession now and find a new ministry in it – call it the male menopause if you like! If it worked, when I was earning sufficient money Barbara would have the offer to do the same. We would both change careers around the age of fifty. But what to do?

I had always been passionate about DIY. When I bought my first motorbike (one pound ten shillings which translates to £1.50) at the age of fifteen when I could only legally ride it around the fields, I soon learned to strip it down and restore it. I built on home extensions of various sorts. I had a phase of building kit cars, and indeed at the time I worked in London I commuted from Kent in a home-built open top sports car with retro running boards, which under the skin was a Ford Cortina. I had restored a couple of Classic cars – an MG Midget for Barbara and a 1950's Humber Estate for me. This last enormous car came as a wreck intercepted for free on its way to the scrapyard. After a year's work I took it on a police skid pan, rode it round Brands Hatch on a Classic Car day, and then six of us took it to Italy for a holiday. I wasn't afraid of using my hands.

After some research I had a plan. The Kent Constabulary had difficulty persuading reluctant double glaziers to come out after midnight to secure premises broken open by criminal damage, accident, paramedics breaking in, police raids, and the like. I got a medium sized van which could take 8ft by 4ft boards and filled it with timber, tools, generator, power tools and the like. Before I finished teaching I offered myself to Kent police for emergency boarding-up from evening to early morning to see if it would work. In the night whilst on the road I visited police stations to introduce myself, eventually distributing six hundred mugs and six thousand pens with my name and number on. Calls began to come in.

Before my teaching job ended Barbara and I, on a whim whilst out shopping, went into an Estate Agent and asked for anything old, unusual and in need of work. We chose a few interesting properties and asked if they were available for viewing. Phone calls were made and just one property had somebody there who could see us. We drove into deepest Kent to a pre-Wealdon Hall House, half of which was for sale. Six weeks later we moved in –

a very unusual scenario at that time. Although the half we bought was built around 1380 and 1420, future research was to turn up an interesting fact. When Sheldwich church was built circa 1070 it was served by monks from Faversham Abbey. But just before the end of the 13th Century the village had its own vicar. Five households contributed to the cost of this – and one was the home we had bought. Well, now it had a vicar living there and, being a mile away from a motorway junction, was perfect for my new job. I could access most of Kent in short time from that junction.

Once I had left teaching I could offer myself to the police 24/7 with the promise to reach almost all of the County within half an hour of a call. It was what they wanted. Over the next ten years they used me on average three hundred and thirty times a year, almost exclusively between the hours of 11.00 pm and 3.00 am. My days were free to follow up customers who wanted me to go back to replace a window or door. Working about half the hours taken up by teaching, I was earning roughly the same money – such is this crazy world in the way it values different types of work and academic achievement! The one-man business had taken off and Barbara was able to change her life too. She left lecturing and retrained as a Counsellor and Psychotherapist, eventually working with GP funded patients and Diocesan clients in addition to private work at home.

Was my new role accessible to Christian ministry: was God there? You bet – in a big way. On a daily basis I was going to meet people in crisis, do something practical for them to meet their immediate need (paid eventually by insurance claim), and offer more than just a bit of boarding up. The police sometimes said they called me because they knew I would be able to help the client more widely – perhaps by my personal approach, perhaps by staying to explain about insurance or victim support. I often got to sudden deaths long before shocked relatives or the Cooperative's 'Private Ambulance' with the body bag, and could help with 'What happens now?' regarding death. I made relationships resulting in people asking me to do other work for them, such as replacing another window where the double glazing seal had broken, allowing it to mist up. It is difficult for the reader to picture just what ministry was there, just how arriving in a Kentish town on a dark, apparently deserted street after the police left – how can this lead to ministry? There follows examples of the situations I was involved in over the three days prior to Christmas Day 1996. Names are changed.

In Dover a shoe shop had its window kicked in, as

did a Furnishing shop in Castle Street – a man was arrested. Miss Patterson in Deal is partly blind and deaf and neighbours were worried. The police and I broke in when she wouldn't answer the telephone or the door. She was ill and needed medical attention. Miss Jones in Folkestone decided to spend Christmas in a nursing home. Her empty bungalow was burgled. On the High Street in Dover the fish and chip shop had a fire which blew out the front shop window: the Astor Secondary School was attacked by vandals. Neighbours in a flat in Augusta Gardens were horrified at finding blood on and around the door. We followed the trail on walls and the floor down three floors and into the street. We broke into the flat and found no clue as to the victim or the cause of wounding. In Tontine Street, Folkestone, a shop had its window kicked in by two drunk fifteen yr olds. From Selborne Street, Margate, Mr Smith had gone to spend Christmas with relatives in Devon: his house was burgled. A similar situation in Sweetgate, Sturry. Ninety year old Mrs Green on Sheppey could not be roused by neighbours. We broke in. She was keeping warm in bed: I stayed to enjoy a ginger wine with her – she looked comical in a very poor wig, worn at an odd angle! Christos, doing English at Canterbury University, was joined by his uncle from Greece and they went to the pub for an hour – enough time to lose one window and sixty

CDs.

Times like that do not just provide opportunities to love one's neighbour in a practical way (and in so doing possibly begin a relationship), but they can be useful sermon fodder. What had these twelve incidents got to do with the real meaning of Christmas that year? Here is the clue, clearly stated to Mary: 'You shall call the child Jesus, for he shall save his people from their sins.' The mini-tragedies I have listed had a connection with sin. Sin needs a remedy. God gave that remedy, and it was the prophet who spelled it out: 'His name shall be called Emmanuel, which means 'God is with us".

There is one known remedy for sin, and it is God with us. This is the theology of Christmas: God speaking in flesh and blood, through Jesus two thousand years ago, and through you now. That's Christmas in one sentence. 'What can I give him, poor as I am? If I were a shepherd I would bring a lamb. If I were a wise man I would do my part. But what I have I bring him – give my heart' – or for that matter, give my skills and love and message of hope. God is our Father precisely because his son is our brother. Wherever we find ourselves, Jesus is there, and whenever we love as he loved, the Word is made flesh.

Being part of the twilight and surreal world of towns

at 2.00 am is a real eye opener. I would arrive, the police would say 'Thanks Mike, there's the damage, we'll leave you to it.' It's all spooky and not a bit scary. Then someone emerges from the shadows. Once they have established that no, you don't have a job for them, and no, you don't need any cannabis, a conversation ensues. At the very lowest level you've been company for them. Other experiences were eye-opening in a shocking way. On May 13th in Dover we broke into an old lady's upper floor flat. The houses were semi-detached with four dwellings, two above and two below in each building, so you were not short of neighbours in the literal way. But this lady was certainly short of neighbours in the Christian sense. We found her seated at her Christmas dinner, very dead. Neighbours said they hadn't seen her for nearly five months but nobody had taken action. Why did we break in? - not over concern for the lady, but because her rent had not been paid. Nobody cared, and folk walked past her door every day ignoring the fact that the inside of the glass was decorated with fake snow and plastic hangings, for Christmas.

Sometimes the call out had its comical side. One police call (I will not shame the police by saying where) said 'meet us at such-an-such an address at a certain time and we want you to break in for us' – surely that is illegal! - ' because you make less mess than we do and can sometimes remove a wrongly fitted double glazing pane without damage.' So I arrive to find a Mercedes van full of about ten officers dressed in black zip-up suits as if they were the SAS. They bundled like bulldozers into the empty property and arrested a rather wizened cannabis plant in a little pot.

Another call was to sort out a broken down door at a certain property. but I was told be to be aware that the owner had a lively Rottweiller. I knocked on what was left of the door. A cartoon figure approached – a bit like Mr Blobby without the pink spots – and suddenly from his rear ran the wretched dog, barking. The dog ran between his legs and jumped at me. The owner caught it mid-flight and I almost had to go home to change my underwear!

On another occasion the break-in was to a disused parish church which had been taken over as an artist's workshop. With head torch and large lamp I made my way around the building at 1.00 am looking for the point of entry. It wasn't easy as brambles had overtaken the graveyard, reminiscent of when heroes battle through with a sword to rescue a Disney maiden in distress. Eventually I found the point of entry - a broken stained glass window under which was a pile of three pallets with an upturned barrow on top. I climbed the rickety steps and shone my light through the aperture, to be confronted by a growling stuffed bear – yes, a real one! Not every encounter therefore provided a need for counselling, unless it were for myself.

Sometimes a customer would ask for all sorts of work on the house and I got to know them well. Significantly most were old folk and I am reminded of my old villagers who say 'I'd love to come to church vicar, but I need to be near a toilet'. Instead of going to church, I went to them. One old couple asked me to witness their will, and asked if I would be offended if the husband gave me five new jackets from the time he was a buyer at Harrods. One was Harris Tweed, two cashmere, two lambswool – and a fine fit they still are!

One call was with a lady whose abusive partner had broken into her home: I finished up replacing several window frames, all the weatherboarding, and chatting a lot. Months later she rang to say she had got back with her partner and had taken a flat in West London, but escaped back home without her car after he beat her up again. Although she could not drive, she did have plenty money, and her partner had bullied her into buying posh cars for him to drive. Her problem was how to get the Rolls Royce (yes, really) back from London. She had contacted firms who wanted £400. I said I'd do it for £100, collected the keys and took a train to London. The car was parked in a fine square overlooked by the lady's apartment in which was her bully. Aware that he might be looking, I quickly snook into the car and then remembered that I had not driven a Rolls before. I had read there was a special way to start them. I looked in the glove compartment and there was a manual. So, press the accelerator three times to set the throttle, insert the key .... I followed instructions only to find the battery was almost dead. On the fifth try and expecting an angry face at the window at any point, the engine fired and I was away!

Mostly the work reflected the commendation of Jesus in saying 'Inasmuch as you did it for one of these, you did it for me'. Mrs X in Folkestone took a long time to come to what was left of her door on Christmas afternoon. She told me she had decided to stay in bed to keep warm. My promotional mug was her only Christmas present. Mr Y had the straight posture of a military man as he met me in his longjohns at 1.30 am. in the bitter cold. There was a hole in the window and, miraculously, the full bottle of milk thrown by a drunken yob had landed on the settee without breaking. Mr Y gripped my forearm and with a tear in his eye said 'This upsets me.

I'm frightened. I'm ninety and nearly blind you know.' I hoovered his carpet to remove the glass he couldn't see. Mr Z died alone in a smart house in Canterbury. The policeman said 'What's it all about? I've spent all night chasing thieves who have to nick other people's stuff. This chap had nice things, but what good are they to him now? We all have to come to this. It makes you think'. This was also at Christmas. A senior officer popped in to see if all was OK – his name was Inspector Gabriel!

All this was unusual ministry, but it really was ministry. I was swimming with the fishes, sharing their environment, talking their language, trying to be *'all things to all men'*. Meanwhile my parish life was splendid because my incumbent was normally comfortable in simply letting me get on with it in my own parish. That was a long and profitable parish ministry. At the age of sixty I stopped boarding up because my teaching pension kicked in: with no mortgage or other debts we had enough money despite a reduced income. So for the ten years before retirement at seventy I was able to play a very full part in parish life indeed, and together we in church achieved a great deal. They had lived with a model of ministry which showed that you did not have to be paid, live in a vicarage and dress in a long black frock to be a proper parish priest. As a result of that about half of my congregation regularly took a formal part in services whether reading, intercessing, leading non sacramental services, and so on. Also, for the first time since being ordained I was able to share fully with my fellow stipendiaries in weekly prayer, chapter meetings and the like which often were organised during working hours.

Chapter three

Churchgoing, Going, Gone?

My chief contention in this chapter is that the church has been digging its own grave for far too long and we need to rethink our image in society, learn how to tell the narrative of God in an increasingly sceptical culture so that that they may glimpse the light of God here on Earth. A first reading this chapter may seem to be negative: I promise more positive sections will follow!

At the General Synod in July 2011 the Church Commissioners were warned that the C of E would cease to be 'functionally extant' in twenty years if the current rate of decline continued. I am reminded of the story of the clergyman who went into his Conference Hotel to check in. A notice in Reception said 'Here we have no problems, only opportunities'. After a short while the vicar returned, referred to the notice and said 'There is a nun in my room: is that a problem or an opportunity?'

Should we view the numerical demise of the C of E as a problem or an opportunity? Is the problem of decline an insoluble crisis which will lead to inevitable death, or is it an opportunity to change? You may know the poem by Philip Larkin, called 'Church Going' from which this extract is taken ....

Once I am sure there's nothing going on
I step inside, letting the door thud shut.
Another church: matting, seats, and stone,
And little books; sprawlings of flowers, cut
For Sunday, brownish now; some brass and stuff ....
Reflect the place was not worth stopping for.

Yet stop I did: in fact I often do,
And always end much at a loss like this,
Wondering what to look for; wondering, too,
When churches fall completely out of use
What we shall turn them into, if we shall keep
A few cathedrals chronically on show,
Their parchment, plate, and pyx in locked cases,
And let the rest rent-free to rain and sheep......................
And what remains when disbelief has gone?
Grass, weedy pavement, brambles, buttress, sky,

A shape less recognizable each week,
A purpose more obscure. I wonder who
Will be the last, the very last, to seek
This place for what it was; one of the crew
That tap and jot and know what rood-lofts were?
Some ruin-bibber, randy for antique ....

I believe we can no longer neglect the increasing
number of people who are quoting statistics which

suggest that the church is on its last legs. They point out that Anglicanism was created as a political expedient when Henry VIII wanted to get rid of Catherine of Aragon, so it's not impossible that its demise will also rest on expedience rather than theology. Between 1971 and 2007, whilst the population of the UK grew 10%, the membership of the Anglican church fell by 43%. The average age of churchgoers is over sixty and rising. It is pointed out with some truth that the core congregation is female, old, posh and rural, and that if the current trend continues there will be no men left by 2027. None of this however denies the spectacular growth of certain churches in this and other countries over recent years – but that is not the problem I address in this book.

Perhaps however there never was a golden age of churchgoing: in 1851 only one third of Londoners ever attended church. So we're not just talking of bringing back lost numbers (which is what many wrongly suggest is required), but of winning people for the first time. It really is mission we should be aiming at rather than maintenance. Under 2% go regularly to their parish church for worship, only 20% of babies are baptised (two thirds in 1950), and even death and marriage are moving out of church. I don't think Anglicanism will disappear, but it cannot stay as it is: as Larkin describes '*a shape less recognisable each week, a purpose more obscure.'*

Certainly the crisis, if genuine, will not go away if we fail to change. It is said that the definition of foolishness is to carry on in the same way in the hope that the outcome might be different next time. So what avenues of change might be worth treading – or are we merely content to wait looking vaguely into the heavens as the disciples did after the Ascension? They were told to stop looking heavenward and get on with the work they had to do which was to baptise people everywhere in the name of the Father, the Son and the Holy Spirit. It's an unusual gift to be able to discern whether any particular route we follow is indeed the will of the Holy Spirit, but at least we should have the faith to get moving – even the best captain cannot guide a ship at anchor. Let's be like St Paul who, travelling in the wrong direction, was prepared to change course when he received a vision of someone calling from elsewhere. We need a courageous effort to think through possible strategies which might be successful in accomplishing the move from maintenance to mission.

Dr Alan Wilson, Bishop of Buckingham, writing in the Church Times, used an interesting way of describing what he believes is needed. First, writing about the Passion narrative he notes that it is *'a story of shaky foundations, a fickle crowd, a puppet governor, professional guardians of the sacred fixed like rabbits in the headlights, well-meaning ecclesiastical politics, scattered and demoralised disciples,'* and at the centre a character asking 'What is truth?' It is a story which resonates perfectly today. In thinking about truth, he quotes Professor Albus Dumbledore of Harry Potter fame, pointing out *'The Truth is a beautiful and terrible thing, and must therefore be treated with great caution.'* The Bishop's suggestion is that the church needs to get real. It needs a reboot, not a bail-out. He wrote that rebooting will not be the end of the church, but its beginning. *'The old dinosaur keels over, as the stale, institutional, sock-puppet-mentality, fantasy C of E PLC dies. The venerable hardware starts up again, reloading afresh lines of core tradition in a form that can be good news on the streets – creation, grace, equality, forgiveness, prayer, love, hope. It gives birth to something less hierarchical and self-obsessed, more akin to a movement than a tired institution. Its values not imposed from above, but animated by passion from the roots up. It celebrates being a dispersed network, not conformity. It seeks to serve, not to manipulate or control. Its gospel is experienced as good news by outsiders.'* I say Amen to that: in fact I should perhaps finish my book now!

Part of my purpose in writing this book is to put up an Aunt Sally: to get us thinking about the possibilities which might be worth exploring, suggest where our current weaknesses lie, and so start a conversation. I have included a good deal of reflection about my personal experience of over forty years ordained, always effectively in charge of at least one church, never taking less than sixty services a year, yet at the same time always being a voluntary minister with a significant ministry in the place of my work. I want to explore the theology of the self-supporting priesthood - a silly name because priesthood won't work unless it's God-supported, but you know what I mean.

I write at a time when Dioceses are waking up to the fact that suddenly they have growing numbers of NSMs, SSMs, OLMs, MSEs, etc. (or is it too revolutionary just to call us 'priests') who are not paid: indeed in some areas we outnumber the paid priests. In passing I should say that if you don't know the full meaning of the list of abbreviations above, you have already got my point – they are not needed and are largely meaningless. Previous books have been written and surveys undertaken about the voluntary ministry, but few have been attempted by someone who like myself has over forty years of personal experience on which to base their perspective, someone with feet in both the parochial system and the world of work outside the parish. My aim is to speak from within my own experience as a volunteer priest gained within the parish church and the workplace.

In very general terms I believe that it is the norm in many congregations that the structure is too clericalised. The result of this is that the ministry of all believers is almost impossibly difficult to realise. There is a long tradition of distrust of clergy, who as a result can feel separated from their flock and lonely. People (not always justly) see clergy as out of touch with national life and thought. My wife, who worked as a Counsellor and Psychotherapist in Cognitive Therapy for diocesan clients, saw many priests who were torn to pieces either by their congregation or their Bishop or both, and failing to cope with the stress experienced as a parish priest. A stipendiary priest, dependent for housing and money on the diocese, working in a situation where (s)he is misunderstood by both parishioners or Bishop, is between a rock and a very hard place indeed. There is no easy prospect of ever achieving much and (s)he does not have other areas of life (such as a paid job) in which to excel. A sincerely meant oath of obedience to one's bishop, made at ordination, can be a source of crushing guilt when things go wrong and he (always a 'he' currently) appears not to be on your side, or even on your wavelength, and has never metaphorically popped his head around your door to ask 'how's it going?' in a friendly way.Not true of all Bishops of course!

An associated problem is that congregations have been encouraged in their habit to leave ministry to their priest, which can paralyse their own instuction to witness. Many Christians in church are highly gifted but their talents are not made available to others because before people are allowed to offer their gift publicly they are given too many formal hurdles to jump – or at least that is what they think.

St Paul points out that 'He gave some to be apostles, some prophets, some evangelists, some pastors and teachers' – a variety of ministerial gifts. All Christians are 'for the perfecting of the saints for the work of ministering, for the building up of the body of Christ.' Ministry is so much more than sacraments offered by a priestly caste. A fundamental question is this: should the parish church members provide the bulk of parish ministry, or should ordained (often paid) Christian ministry provide it – or both? The current balance sees the church defined by the nature of its ministry. Many a churchgoer has been made to feel that they are not allowed even to pray together unless a priest is there to 'offer prayer' for them – this is nonsense. I have seen situations during interregna when rural churches close their doors on some Sundays because 'there is nobody to take the service'. The laity hugely underestimate their ability to lead and share a rich worship experience.

I want in this book to ask the question 'Is the church's mission being held back by our buildings, our organisation and our theology? Do the current administrative, training and financial systems serve us well today?' Is it time to reassert the theology of the priesthood of all believers, and if this were done would Christians then be given the confidence to 'be priests' in the world of work? I overstate the case here to make a point, but God was 'in Christ, reconciling the world to himself' yet our systems lock God up in (usually) old buildings for an hour a week. We should encourage Christian ministry away from church. After all, those in church have ready access to ministry. We need to fish beyond the little church pond, in the murky waters of secular society.

Some thoughts on the secularisation of society...... It is common to meet the opinion, from people who have not met the Prince of Peace that religion is a source of division and fighting. Those who share a spiritual perspective maintain that materialism and other aspects of modern society have caused people to lose touch with personal religious faith, which was (still is?) deeply embedded in much of our culture. This loss has impoverished people; secularisation has caused untold damage. The world is ill with disillusionment: having tried to believe in Man instead of God, and found Man wanting, they are now unable to believe in either God or Man. How has the church allowed this to happen? For hundreds of years, our culture was saturated with religious values. But somehow the church has allowed life and religion to become separated in peoples' understanding. There are those (see below) who contend that Christianity and religion have been separated. This leads to statements such as 'you can be a Christian without going to church', or 'I know churchgoers who don't act like Christians' – true but used here as a means of dismissing the validity of faith.

The marginalisation of religion has left a vacuum, dissatisfaction, dysfunctional relationships. People feel let down, not valued. Perhaps the world has changed and the church has failed to adapt quickly enough to that change. The Reformers used a phrase 'Ecclesia semper reformunda est' – the church is continually in need of renewal: but we have ignored that. Outsiders see the church as characterised by boundaries and control. Often liturgy ('the work of the people') turns out to be a solo performance to a paying audience: people think church is about what happens in a special building. So our church needs more fuzzy edges than it currently has. We need open borders to let in the inadequate and the hesitant, to discern glowing embers of faith and fan them into fire, to welcome those who feel unworthy.

The Bible tells us that the common people heard Jesus gladly: part of our problem is that the vast majority of church culture is not in the hands of common people. So some dismiss faith not on theological grounds or points of belief but because they find incongruity in the claim that the church is for ordinary folk yet perceive it's hierarchy as untouched by the daily experience of ordinary folk. Those of us who rub shoulders with the hierarchy know that this is simply not true, but communicating that fact seems to be beyond our ability.

It's not that religion has been tried and found wanting: it isn't even tried any more. People treat the church not so much as untrue, but irrelevant to them. It's fair to say that most people in the UK still think of themselves as Christian, but they have decided that their Christianity doesn't need the church any more. Church membership has become optional to their Christianity. Churchgoers however believe that it is primarily through the church that Christ's work is done, his gospel proclaimed, and see the church not as a voluntary organisation but a living organism through which God is acting today.

In the 1930's Dietrich Bonhoeffer suggested that the church could become the custodian not of faith but of religion. Perhaps that has happened. How many people come to their vicar for hatching, matching or dispatching with the phrase 'I'm not religious but ....'? Perhaps it is the perceived threshold of religion and not the threshold of faith which keeps people away. We need to ask the question 'Why is it that Joe Public has a formula in his head which sees Jesus as good and religion as bad?' I have frequently heard people blame 'religion' for countless ills, but it is almost unknown for them to blame Jesus by name. This is a formula for confusion and misunderstanding. I think it was Martin Buber who wrote 'Religion hides God.' Perhaps people think that religion is alright if it is kept in place and not allowed to interfere with people's lives!

An American rapper called Jefferson Bethke has written a rap entitled 'Why I hate religion but love Jesus'. If you view it on You Tube you will be joining over 2 million others who have already done that. I print an extract below, not because I think all he says is correct, but to illustrate the sort of view which I am sure many share. Try to read it with a rap beat – it helps!

I mean if religion is so great, why has it started so many wars. Why does it build huge churches, but fails to feed the poor. See the problem with religion, is it never gets to the core. It's just behaviour modification, like a long list of chores. Like lets dress up the outside make look nice and neat. But it's funny that's what they use to do to mummies while the corpse rots underneath. Now I ain't judging, I'm just saying quit putting on a fake look. Cause there's a problem if people only know you're a Christian by your Facebook. Because if grace is water, then the church should be an ocean. It's not a museum for good people, it's a hospital for the broken. Which means I don't have to hide my failure, I don't have to hide my sin. Because it doesn't depend on me it depends on him. See because when I was God's enemy and certainly not a fan. He looked down and said   I......want ....that ....man. Which is why Jesus hated religion, and for it he called them fools. Don't you see so much better than just following some rules. Now let me clarify, I love the church, I love the Bible, and yes I believe in sin. But if Jesus came to your church would they actually let him in. See remember he was called a glutton, and a drunkard by religious men. But the son of God never supports self righteousness not now, not then. Now back to the point, one thing is vital to mention. How Jesus and religion are on opposite spectrum. See one's the work of God, but one's a man made invention. See one is the cure, but the other's the infection. See because religion says do, Jesus says done. Religion says slave, Jesus says son. Religion puts you in bondage, while Jesus sets you free. Religion makes you blind, but Jesus makes you see. And that's why religion and Jesus are two different clans. Religion is man searching for God, Christianity is God searching for man.

There is of course a dilemma here which needs spelling out. Some will point out that religion is by nature other-worldly. Our liturgy is sometimes at its best when it points us towards experiences of holiness, of transcendence. Many Christians welcome the benefit of a silent retreat and others find great help from entering a cloistered religious community which is a very different model to the lives of most people. So you could argue that there should be evidence of separation between those with faith and those without. In that sense Christians should be different, religious worship is by nature unusual.

But the other side of this coin of faith is that in order to explain to us exactly what he is like, God always becomes flesh. What I mean is that our faith is incarnational – God became flesh in the person of Jesus Christ who chooses to work through the flesh and blood of his followers today. Most (admittedly not all) people first encounter Jesus Christ in relationship with another person. How can the expression of our faith be at the same time incarnational (earthy) and heavenly – and have we sometimes got that balance wrong? Why have we become so detached from common life, apparently aloof to the very people we seek to love into the Kingdom? It cannot be just that we are too 'churchy', that our conversation is more boring than anything else, that we are too introverted, so narrow that we think the vicar's latest chasuble is deeply important …. Is it?

Are those of us who go to church so separate that we breathe an artificial atmosphere and are unable to reach over the barrier into the daily lives of ordinary people; to make our journey attractive enough so that they want to join us? Certainly we are accused of being engrossed with secondary issues and self preservation. Yet we claim that our task in the world is to be genuinely self-forgetful in order to enable us to respond in love to our neighbour. Authentic Christianity demonstrates love for God and love for neighbour: indeed the first can be said to be absent unless the second is real. I will suggest later that the current church by some of its practice, organisation and leadership can be counter-productive in enabling us to demonstrate love of neighbour.

At times our witness is such that the neighbour we hope to love is blinded from being able to grasp the essence of faith because religion has got in the way. I say 'I believe in God' but my neighbour hears 'I am so afraid of life that I hold on to a fantasy of imaginary wish-fulfilment of life elsewhere and meanwhile hide in the institution of the church'. In a secular society Christians have to find an authentic way of stressing that we believe in the wonder and value of the real world and in a fulfilled life here and now. We are courageous enough to commit our life to Jesus Christ who offers freedom, life and redemption which is creative and triumphant in this world and not just the next. We're not trying to escape from anything!

What's more we need to find a way of showing them that we do not usually discover faith through the imposition of the views of clerical authority: we are not believing what we are told to believe by someone else who was in turn told what to believe. Our faith is our own discovery. The expression of our theology in daily relationship must emphasise not law but grace: we have to find ways of including people rather than looking for ways to exclude them. Let us avoid the triviality of 'churchyness' and share things which are really important to God. Jesus did not found a society, prescribe its organisation and lay down its statutes. He lived alongside twelve people for three years and then left them to get on with the mission he had modelled. You can argue that the church was created following the gift of the Holy Spirit at Pentecost, but I believe that in essence it was there as soon as Jesus had his few special followers gathered around him: the church is a continuum from that tiny initial group who learned faith through friendship with Jesus, and grew in knowledge of God as 'our Father'.

So I think we need to ask if some of the secularisation of society is a result of the institutional church forgetting the fundamentals, presenting instead a model of a highly organised and hierarchical system which imposes complex financial and administrative procedures, rigid legal precedent and strong tradition. Jesus' own words that 'you, because of your tradition, have made void the word of God' is a warning we should heed, if it is not too late. Will we awaken peoples' faith with remote, impersonal institutions, or with intimate spontaneity? Organisation can quench Spirit, but this is not inevitable – we can learn to adopt a more appropriate model. Can we rediscover the language of Galilee instead of the official voice of mother church, and if we can, would this positively attract our sceptical secular society?

Perhaps we should demonstrate the belief that in one sense Jesus was not the final word: he promised his followers that they would do even greater things that he did. God's work is continuous and never finished: an adventurous growth rather than a fixed-in-tradition institution. We can only realise this if we look out to the world more than we look inwards at the system. To read the press you would believe that the church is introverted, preoccupied with its own security and remote to real life. We know that isn't true, but who's to blame for that view? In the end the institutional view is secondary and derivative but we manage to make it appear to be fundamental to faith. Our questions will not normally be best served by an approach which is primarily archaeological. Did not someone once say that those willing to lose their lives are the very ones who will save them? It is dangerously unhealthy to keep asking how we can save the institutional church, instead of looking out towards others and how to save them.

Authentic Christianity shouts the good news that 'This is eternal life: to know the only true God and Jesus Christ whom he has sent.' The centre of faith is God, not the church. Surely the fault has been ours that the world does not appreciate this. Why should they, when so often the church appears to be a pretty anachronism to be given an outing from time to time when people want to marry or be buried (especially if that is a national event, which we 'do' extraordinarily well), or appears to operate in the background striving to resist the inevitable tide of change. The church too often shouts 'this is what you ought to do' when it should be demonstrating 'this is what God is like.' As a result people reject the church and are not given the opportunity to make an informed decision about whether to reject God or not because we have confused them about what is important.

I have no detailed blueprint of exactly how we can repair past damage and put Christ back into people's perception of Christianity. In the end this is the work of the Holy Spirit – but He works through you and me. But I do know that we cannot go on pretending to our neighbour that the essence of faith is devotional observance and correct personal conduct as set down in church law. Come on! - some of the best Christians I have known are not regular churchgoers. Liturgical exercises are very helpful to Christians but they are not the focus of what God requires of us. Of course we all know churchgoers who by their conduct and views are damaging to the image of Christianity, and that will always be the case. As Jesus said, it is the sick who need a doctor, not people who are well. If you go into hospital you expect to find sick people: if you go to church you find some damaged people, hopefully looking for a way to find repair. I remember a man who regularly went to hear a wonderful (and long-winded) evangelical Welsh minister in a large congregation in London, who one day said to me 'I come every week to hear his wonderful oratory: of course I don't believe a word of it'! We cannot let such people be the only image of churchgoers that some folk like to adopt. A stranger coming into church should see that we believe in resurrection, in every sense. They should be in the presence of sincerity, spontaneity, an attractive atmosphere full of constructive hope. They should not feel that here is a group of people preoccupied with the survival of their peculiar machinery.

Chapter Four

In the Beginning...

Christianity grew out of Judaism, yet it never really took root and flourished in Jewish soil. As you read of the growth of the new faith it soon becomes clear that it was being established by people like St Paul in non-Jewish provinces where it quickly flourished. Even the twelve apostles, except Peter and John, soon leave their home stage in the biblical account, rather than sticking with the traditional system. The faith advanced in the industrial centres of population which were on established trade routes – Antioch, Ephesus, Thessalonica, Rome, Corinth. The early evangelists seem to have chosen to work in areas where busy people were living out their secular lives, and there they gave them a practical faith which made sense of their experiences.

One could argue that Christianity grew because it was not purely spiritual and subjective (which is more the characteristic of a sect) but based on love of neighbour. The early evangelists poured scorn on 'religion' as such, preaching that the fruit of the Spirit is socially based – it's about ethics and morals and behaviour in addition to belief. They spoke ill of the law of the old religion, saying that the past rules were now replaced by one law, that of love, which had mastery over all circumstances which arise in the life of the Christian follower. The new faith was proved in works based on love of neighbour and in enhancing life 'in all its fullness'.

So in some ways the early church emphasis was not the promotion of machinery to save souls, but a passion to redeem corporate society in a way which brought fullness of life to people. Not a new club for religious people, but the birth of a group who in their lives modelled the very nature of God's character; a model of love so attractive that onlookers would say 'I want that for myself too.' The new movement built itself up in love and found focus in the Eucharist as an exhibition of agape in action. Christian faith was about a redeemed society growing out of individual personal redemption. Christians still lived within the world, and it was very important that they should, but within that world they acted like a distinct society existing within a different tradition. Christianity was the social ethic of this new religion but it could (can) only grow by living and working alongside non-believers who are viewed as neighbours to be loved into a fuller life. This movement was not just for those who sought to formally study theology, this was for the common person. Early evangelists did not separate themselves from common humanity: they worked within all groups of people to attract them into becoming fellow pilgrims walking the way of faith.

Surprisingly little is written about any formal hierarchy in the new movement. Direct communication could be made between people of flesh and the God made flesh, without endless special mediators who in some past manifestations seemed to suggest that their intervention between God and humans was through magical procedures. The people are offered joy, peace and a new freedom from endless laws – no wonder it spread rapidly. The new faith went beyond a narrow religion, emphasising that everyone is made in the Creator's image whatever their gender, race or creed, enabling their approach to the whole of Creation to be transformed. No wonder, centuries later, so many people who gained fame from scientific achievement were also those who had a Christian faith, which opened them up to the wonders of nature.

We need to recover in our teaching the primary importance of love for neighbour as the very ground of our 'religion'. Love dictates the best behaviour in every culture. Jesus did not attempt to lay down endless rules of behaviour for each generation to follow in an ever changing world. What would be the value of laws for circumstances which had not even arisen until generations later. Do we need a clear biblical rule on matters such as the use of nuclear power, assisted death, stem cell use, genetic modification, climate change, and so on, and so on? You won't find much about those things from the mouth of Jesus! But his law of love enables sensible and appropriate principles to be formulated from that fundamental law of love. We can never decide what is right or wrong in every situation by quoting a specific saying of Jesus, but his law of love exposes motive, penetrates the heart, provides a redeemed judgement providing the route towards the answer to every such question. When you look at answers Jesus gave to enquirers they often prove to be particular and local: for instance not every rich young ruler has to sell all he has and give to the poor, 'though it could be argued that 'follow me' is good counsel every time. What is eternal in his approach is the principle of love.

I have seen many 'WWJD?' armbands and badges, or even (on a protester's tent outside St Paul's Cathedral during an anti-capitalist rally) the full quotation 'What Would Jesus Do?'. But I wonder if the more appropriate question to a particular problem is 'What Will I Do?' The appearance of God in the flesh of Jesus Christ is a disclosure which has a historical limitation. It happened in a specific social and economic climate, a definite place and time. It therefore is not the case that in a literal sense we can presume to copy Jesus, because the situation in which we live is unique to here and now. What we can and must do is to show our commitment by loving as he loves. 'Christ left us an example that we should follow in his steps' - central to our discipleship is to speak and act in love.

Since his day the world has changed. Our thoughts and feelings, our understanding of morality, is so different from two thousand years ago. Whole tracts of human life and interest were unknown to Jesus in his fleshly time. As far as we know he was celibate, he was not dominated by economics and consumerism, he never used Google and did not have an iPad. Part of the very essence of his incarnation is that he was limited, he 'emptied himself'. If we now lived exactly as Jesus did, using the same words, this would not be true discipleship. To follow Jesus is not to copy him, but to translate his spirit into our current situation in very different circumstances, and we can do that because of the indwelling of the Holy Spirit. So it would be wrong to look for renewal today in terms of a resuscitation of past ways of doing and speaking: God is creative and is to be experienced in new ways, as the needs of generations change. But in every time and place the unmistakable and convincing characteristic of a follower of Christ has been agape in addition to faith – this is what Christianity must demonstrate. A tree is known by its fruits, and the authentic fruit of Christianity is love.

I have laboured this point to suggest a paradox: that in one sense Jesus was not just concerned with the conduct of each person, but also with the supreme task of redeeming the relationship of all humankind to God. By finding again our true nature as a child of God and siblings of one another, we shall know the Kingdom of God; a kingdom out of time, in eternity. Jesus' purpose was not primarily to reform our morals but to show us what God is like, and to help us discover the joy of family likeness.

Imagine what Jesus, with his heroism and knowledge and insight, might have done, and here I am reminded of the temptations to which he was exposed following his baptism. He could have led his people to a political freedom and presided over a golden age, but he saw such things as the voice of the devil. He was not that sort of Messiah. His work was to be born into our human situation where he would demonstrate what truth and freedom look like in the new kingdom outside space and time, and meanwhile model how to be like him whilst here on Earth. By his modelling of the nature of God, He at the same time modelled the true nature of redeemed people, and how we should live with one another.

I will say more later about how I believe that the theology of incarnation, particularly as expressed in the priesthood of all believers, is not sufficiently evident in the expression of the church in the 21st Century. The way in which the early church might have been founded, evolved and structured could still challenge our current practice and organisation which seems to work differently to that of the first Christians. We should question whether a reminder of earlier patterns might suggest that we have gone wrong and what we need to change.

Chapter Five

Going to Church or Being the Church?

This chapter questions whether the church institution places limits on Christian witness and discourages the freedom necessary for people to exercise their gifts. There is confusion in the minds, especially of non churchgoers, about the interface between 'church' and Christianity. Somehow we need to clarify the concept that Christianity is not just represented by church buildings. Success for us depends on what Christians say and do in their daily lives. We each must remember that we might be the only 'gospel' some people will ever read.

Some churchgoers when asked about how being a Christian makes a difference to their lives, would answer in terms of religion. They might say 'I go to church; I pray.' Further probing might elicit that they avoid naughty behaviour, regularly go to Holy Communion, or even that they pay their church quota. To be fair, Christianity does of course have a religious content; we observe certain obligations and duties within 'the church', worship, prayer, devotion, fellowship – these things are helpful and necessary. But it is interesting that few Christians would initially talk of themselves as *being* the church. More than that, some clergy actively encourage their congregation to leave behind the world - the workplace, the garden, the golf course - in order to 'give time to God.' If so, what on earth do they think people have been doing all day!

If God is not present in the richness of 'ordinary' life, then I can't imagine where he is! Isn't the fact that God is present in the world the cornerstone of our faith - what incarnation is about? The popular cook Delia Smith, has said: *'Religion seems to be moving away from the rest of life, whereas God is present in the warp and woof of everyday living.'* We recognise God in the whole of life. We need to remind Christians that life outside of the church building is not an alternative to Christian life, but is where Christian life needs to be lived.

There are many ways in which, to the outsider, the church seems not to be connected to their experience. It might for instance be because we speak an unusual language. A stranger coming into church might feel that many of the phrases we use are strange – we march together as pilgrims, wash in blood, sing songs of Zion, and so on. It could be that an outsider expecting the emphasis in church to be towards worship and love of neighbour, instead experiences a group whose main concern appears to be the maintenance of a mediaeval building, or some other target which seems to be totally divorced from what we know as mission. They might find a congregation which sits through the service like theatre critics, offering their judgements over coffee later.

Bishop Graham Cray has likened some churches to a whirlpool which sucks people into their peculiar culture, when it ought to be a launch pad to equip people for whole life discipleship. In other words, the true church is missional when it is fulfilling its purpose. Another problem in rural churches (most of my ministry) is that church buildings are often not where people live any more. Perhaps they were before the Black Death wiped out the villagers around the church and their homes fell into decay and disappeared, but the church building is not where the newer homes were built. Other church buildings are where they are because they were built not to the glory of God so much as the glory of the local lord or other benefactor. One might hope if the building is not physically central, then at least the human church – it's members – are busy being incarnational within the community at home, at their place of work, school, shopping centre, etc. But is there evidence that is the case?

A way forward in some inner city churches has been to get away from the church building specifically to enable Christians to live and witness alongside people who would never think of entering a church. It's called incarnational mission: one model is to have teams of Christians choosing to live in city estates in order to witness there as literal neighbours. It's like the early missionaries – going into a culture where the people are almost totally ignorant of the fundamental tenets of faith, and sharing it with them through words and living. The focus is not on preaching, but on sharing lives together. This imitates the life of Jesus: in the words of 'The Message' translation of John's gospel: 'The Word became flesh and blood, and moved into the neighbourhood.' Although they might not verbalise it in this way, people who have always experienced the church coming at them from a place of power and influence, enjoy the novelty and respond more readily to shared experience, listening and discovering in the place where they are. The church people have not said 'Come to us', but rather 'let us go to them.'

When I was training for Ordination in the Diocese of Southwark in the 1960's, our weekend training was in Wychcroft in Surrey. In the chapel behind the altar there was a painting of Christ the Worker, Jesus wearing a carpenter's apron. About half of the ordinands there were called to a stipendiary ministry, about half to a self-supporting ministry. For the Self Supporting Ministers the idea of Jesus as a working carpenter was powerful. But more memorable to me was that at the end of every Eucharist the Principal would dismiss us by saying 'Now go out and be the leaven in the lump!' I felt strongly that 'in the lump' was where I had to be to share my faith, this was how I must fulfil my particular calling. Even now I find that phrase stronger than the modern exhortation to 'Go in peace, to love and serve the Lord'. The teaching implied in such sayings is that you cannot leaven society unless you are in it. If you are living the same life, sharing the same difficulties, gains and pressures as your neighbour, then it is often easier to make your faith real to others.

We must not get possessive about God – he is not the private property of religion or the religious. He is working, still creating, still 'making all things new' in the world and every person is very much his concern. There is not a single person who is not important to God. Christians must not speak and act in relation to people outside the church as if they are somehow less important to God. Within the church we must not suggest that men are more important than women, that clergy are more important than laity, and so on. We are too ready to pretend that God belongs to churchgoers, and anyone else who happens to tick particular boxes of belief and practice. This attitude of exclusivity has been disastrous when we have applied it to our buildings as if they belong only to regular worshippers, as I now suggest below.

Chapter Six

Are Our Church Buildings Frustrating Christian Mission?

Most of our church plant is of major national, architectural and historical importance. When people talk about 'the church in our parish' they are usually referring to the building rather than the presence of a worshipping community. In my village of five hundred people, 78% list themselves as 'Christian' but that doesn't mean there are three hundred and ninety worshippers: even self-confessed Christians use the word church to mean the building. But the days when that building belonged to the community in any real sense are long gone. Hence, in a recent national survey in which people were asked 'Where is your place of peace and well-being?', the answer 'church' came 22nd – Oh dear!

I will exaggerate, but imagine a church building just a few hundred years ago: a wonderfully flexible and useful resource to a village community: good for teaching, settling disputes, barn dances, village celebrations and the like. Most villagers play their part in working or donating to maintain it in good order. There would be festivals several times a year which spilled out onto the streets. Then imagine (it isn't difficult!) that a few religious decide they want the building for themselves. They severely restrict its usefulness by fixing rows of seats (uncomfortable at that) to the floor. People who come to church confess to be a fellowship, but it's an odd fellowship which sits in rows looking at the back of someone else's neck. They label some of the seats as reserved for particular persons where others may not go (the most amusing example I know is the church on the hill near Whitby Abbey, with pews for Church Maids, Strangers, Visitors, etc.). Some people stop going because it's not comfortable, or warm, or well lit, or welcoming, or does not have a toilet – they go off to build a village hall for non religious activities and the social centre of the community goes elsewhere.

After a few generations the minority religious find the building impossible to finance. Appeals to villagers are not very successful because they don't need the church building any more They don't use it much except for occasional offices and have gained the impression that it's not theirs anyway - unless you threaten to close it of course!

When I became priest of my last village church – a potentially wonderful 11th Century building, it was being used by a dozen older people for one hour a week, and they locked the door as they left. One side chapel had been unused for nearly a century and was being slowly ingested by a myriad of creatures with and without legs, and by damp. That space alone cost almost £50,000 just to get a sound shell which we could then make useful as a general purpose meeting room with kitchen facilities. A sister church had a notice on the entry to the North aisle with the message 'Danger: falling masonry'. None of the five mediaeval churches in our cluster had a toilet: twenty three years later just one has a toilet, in a former mortuary building in the graveyard. Only one church had a water tap (cold) supplying water inside the building (though one had a supply inside the tower.) Only one church had central heating, one had gas heaters mounted high on the pillars, the other three no heating. What on earth had possessed my predecessors to make them think these things did not matter?

Churchgoers are in a quandary – is it their building, or does it belong to the whole community? The question of ownership is not straightforward to say the least. The situation is something like this - information gleaned from an internet search. The church, churchyard and minister's houses are not owned by the corporate or central body of the church of England, nor by the Diocese, nor by the PCC. Most are held in trust by the incumbent, not for the congregation but for the parish.

The parish can use the properties with strings attached by the C of E. Because the buildings are held on behalf of the people, their disposal and transfer has to be regulated by Parliament, under very strict rules. Churchwardens hold in trust the moveable bits of the church by warrant of their office. As seen occasionally, when a congregation is in dispute with its Bishop they can be thrown out of the building they have built and paid for. I can think of no more crazy arrangement for proper care of this extraordinary heritage. Are you any clearer now who owns the church buildings? - I thought not!

If the Diocese owned the building (and to muddy the waters they might be partly responsible for just one section of it, such as the chancel) then the churchgoers would ask them for help. But they don't own it. In any case this doesn't work because the finances flow in the other direction – the Diocese levies significant costs annually (called the Parish Share) to the people to worship there. The congregation may be fortunate enough to get financial support from a government body to help with repairs, yet they are always aware that parishes pay back in VAT more than the total grants awarded nationally by English Heritage.

If the churchgoers owned the building they would want to adapt it to make it fit for purpose within their community – a purpose much richer than just a place for weekly worship. But they don't own it. If they did they might consider putting the building back into the heart of village activities. Their wish-list might include getting rid of the pews so the space is more flexible, a disabled toilet with baby changing facilities, adaptation to cater for disabilities, good heating and lighting, redecoration, an office with a telephone, WiFi, a kitchen – the list goes on. But the churchgoers don't own the place and the Diocese can seem very reluctant to allow change despite the fact that earlier generations seem to have remodelled the building to suit their needs in past centuries. To formally request a change (applying for a Faculty) costs a couple of hundred pounds just to ask the question.

This sort of difficulty has led to a very odd situation. A very small percentage of the population has been made responsible for looking after nationally important buildings which they do not own and over which they have minimal control. Of the fourteen thousand five hundred places of worship listed as being of special historical or architectural interest, 85% are maintained by Church of England members. The C of E uses about sixteen thousand churches and forty two cathedrals and its members spend £100 million a year on repairs alone. I suggest that most of the members would prefer to use their money in more people-based activities.

These members do a heroic job. The same few people do a huge amount of unpaid work for their churches, and in addition give over seventy two million hours of voluntary work every year for social initiatives outside the church – an estimated contribution of £1.5 billion, and give £50 million annually to other charities. Church members provide half of the parent and toddler support groups in the UK. They provide the biggest network of debt counselling and in the coming year expect to feed one hundred thousand hungry people through one hundred and seventy food banks. These figures were quoted by Dr Krish Kandiah at Spring Harvest in 2012. This situation is not trumpeted, is little known or celebrated, but this needs to be said: it is a fantastic accomplishment year after year.

Increasingly those same people are reluctant to carry on maintaining a building. Why? - because they would rather be doing Christianity than doing church maintenance. Look again at the figures above: twice as much spent on buildings than is given to other charities. That cannot be justified.

Let me now move into a fantasy world. Consider my current village church: a building almost a thousand years old, with about thirty members on the electoral roll, of which ten are wage earners. The annual costs they bear for the building includes approximately £3000 Parish Share, £10,000 running expenses (gas, electricity, maintenance, etc.) and £2,500 to keep the churchyard tidy. Like many villages, we no longer can find a permanent organist, but we do have a couple of people who can each play once a month. Our organ tuning is about £400 a year which in our case works out at over £4 a hymn – it all adds up. Because I am a voluntary minister, ministry costs are about £500 rather than the £40,000 cost of stipend plus on-costs. (Correction – this week I have been told the true cost of a stipendiary is nearer £60,000). On top of this we have tried to enhance our facilities to make the building more useful to the wider village and have needed to undertake major repair work from time to time – cost averaging £10,000 a year. In round figures then, £500 ministry, £25,000 for building and the Diocese each year.

That's the situation typical of many parishes. Now to indulge my fantasy. One of two things happens. Perhaps the cost of this nationally important building is taken on by the nation and it is saved. Alternatively my current congregation says 'This makes no Christian sense. We'll lock the door, send the key to the Diocese, cancel our membership by not signing up when the electoral role comes up for renewal. Then on paper there will not be any C of E members in the village. We can worship God in the Village Hall, using the same service booklets. That way we'll be able to spend our money differently. Let's be realistic and try to save about £15,000 of what we used to spend. What shall we do with that? We could split it thee ways and support local, national and international charities.'

Locally, £5,000 a year could go to the Children's' Hospice, or Air Ambulance, or a children's playground in the village, or to enhance our environment – village trees on the Green, benches, flower beds, facilities for the elderly, village notices, etc.

Nationally we could give £5,000 to medical research for Cancer, Alzheimers, Arthritis, send it to Help for Heroes, etc.

Internationally, for overseas countries we could choose to buy one of these: five thousand chickens each laying two hundred eggs a year, four hundred bag gardens to grow vegetables to give three meals a day, four hundred fruit trees, two hundred and fifty fuel saving stoves, one hundred beehives, one hundred and fifty goats, twenty water stores, etc.' Every year.

All this from one village of two hundred dwellings! What if lots of church groups over the nation did that? As a Christian, if you were given the option to spend money on the building or on people, which would you prefer to do if it were possible? Would you at least like the choice? If you were not a Christian, how impressed would you be by a small group making such a huge difference to the lives of people in the world. Buildings or people: which would you choose? Sadly there isn't a choice – is there? Yes, I'm living in cloud-cuckoo-land to think such a thing is possible – aren't I?

But leaving my fantasy, it is unreasonable to ask to what extent the cost of looking after the nation's built heritage is severely limiting the energy and witness of churchgoers? Which model is more Christ-like? Me? I'd like a compromise. I'd like the nation to cough up the money for maintenance, repair and help towards making the building useful to the village. The Parish Council could pay for maintenance of the churchyard and other land by a tiny levy on the Council Tax. Lottery money over a decade could bring the buildings up to more modern standards of energy use, etc. The worshippers could use it for worship (say, a fee of £50 an hour) and manage the plant, villagers could use it for commercial rates. The building is saved, useful, back at the centre of

109

village life, loved. Is something like that too much to dream? Come on – this village has no pub or shop or garage, no Post Office, no street lights or main drainage, and an occasional bus which serves route 666! Is it too much for the villagers to ask for their church building back, and for churchgoers to be freed to be creatively generous with their money?

A few statistics to offer a perspective. Britain's annual military defence budget at £33.7 billion is the third or fourth largest in the world. That works out at £648,076,923 a day. The C of E has sixteen thousand churches (about fourteen thousand four hundred listed). One week's defence budget would give every church an average of £40,505 to spend on the building. It wouldn't take many weeks to put them all in good repair, useful to the community would it! OK I know it will not happen, but I can dream!

Chapter Seven

What Has Theology to Say About Our Current Ministry?

If we accept that God's redemptive purpose is for all people, all times and all creation, this must inform the pattern of our mission and be reflected in our liturgy. I suggest that it is counter productive to present the faith in restrictive or negative ways: for instance to suggest that we should appear to be relatively unconcerned with our wonderful world, devaluing its richness and worth. Faith should not restrict our interest, but expand it.

This means avoiding the sort of worship which appears to the outsider as a barren formality, institutional. God is alive, real, near, interested in every facet of our lives, doing new things, still creating. To reflect this we must look for more spontaneity and colour in our liturgy, encouraging worshippers to take a much more active part in the experience. If people judge that the worship experience we offer is largely irrelevant to their life and values, they will find it unattractive. Telling the historical story of God publically in predominately Jewish terms such as that expressed by Psalms and Hebraic canticles is fine, but more is needed to catch the interest of the new worshipper. Christian faith is based on the promised

111

salvation of God through Jesus Christ, but God has not finished his creative work in the world. Worship needs to stress the present and future work of the Holy Spirit. Christian experience is not exclusively mediated by tradition and past history, therefore our liturgy must clearly express what God is doing today (and of course some of it does).

In my ordained ministry I have led Eucharists using the Prayer Book, the 1928 Prayer Book, Series One, Series Two, Series Three, the Alternative Service Book and Common Worship, in addition to a few experimental versions. So the attempt to drag the liturgical experience into a more modern expression appears to have been very active. Similarly, I have on my bookshelves at least nine versions of the Bible – as a child this was certainly not possible. I applaud all this, but wonder sometimes whether the revisers have clear aims in what they are attempting to do, because occasionally it looks as if they are making minor changes (e.g. inclusive language, which is fine) but missing the mark in terms of engaging new Christians. God is not just a God of the past and we need to ensure that our offer in worship is not dictated primarily by tradition, expediency and circumstances.

Chapter Eight.

How Did the Early Church Grow?

*' .... the churches were strengthened in the faith
and increased in numbers daily.'*

We read that within a few years of the Crucifixion, the world was turned upside down by the new Christians. Can we learn from the early missionary method – St Paul being the supreme practitioner of apostolic ministry – or has the passage of two millennia made it obsolete? How did it happen? The circumstances for Paul were certainly very different to today, but perhaps the principles of his method have lasting value.

Roland Allen was a missionary in North China. One hundred years ago, in a book titled 'Missionary Methods: St Paul's and Ours' he had this to say about Paul:

'He had no preconceived plan of campaign: he went where the Spirit led; he sought for the open doors ..... he aimed definitely at converting men and women to faith in Christ: we never find him simply preparing the ground for future conversions. Then he planted churches which rapidly became self-supporting and self-governing.

In about six months he has founded the church, taught the converts the necessary elements of the faith, ordained a ministry and made provision for the administration of the sacraments. Then St Paul passes on elsewhere, and the church is left to grow by the power of the Holy Spirit. He occasionally visits it, writes to it and sends to it his fellow workers; but in no case does he settle down to govern it ....

Again, in his teaching St Paul is content to lay down simple and strong foundations. He does not attempt to give it the elaborate teaching which is thought necessary in a modern mission. Once more in the exercise of discipline, St Paul strives to inspire a spirit, not to enforce a law. He carefully abstains from imposing upon his churches any external code of authority. His object is not to compel them to obey a law, but to lead them to obey the inner guidance of the Holy Spirit.

Then, lastly, his ideal of unity is essentially spiritual. It is not based upon organisation, but upon life. He makes no attempt to bind them all into one by any centralised organisation or by obedience to a common authority, but by the power of one spirit and one life. We neglect open doors .... we found churches and keep them in leading strings for a hundred years, and even then are not within measurable distance of giving them independence.'

How do we respond to this? Are modern church leaders too ready to *'keep them in leading strings'*, to have too many codes of authority; too cautious to allow more local independence (especially in terms of training and employing local ministry)? In this sense, has the current organisation insufficient faith to give churches sufficient freedom to be led by the Spirit?

Am I unusual in wanting freedom – freedom to make mistakes and to succeed, and to take responsibility for the outcome? From an early age I think that freedom has been central to my needs. One of my earliest memories was formed when I was about four years old. Every Christmas before then, my parents had made my Christmas presents – money was in very short supply. But that year they managed to scrape together enough to buy me a tricycle, new or second-hand. I understand that at four in the morning on 25th December I woke up my parents by riding round their bed, ringing the bell and shouting 'He's been!' That three wheeler gave me new freedom. Later, I used that freedom by running away from home: except that I don't think that was my intention. It was just the joy of freedom. I was discovered a mile from home still pedalling away! At the back of my mind I knew my parents would be able to find me and bring me home because that is what parents do. My adventure was a mixture of freedom and complete trust. What a metaphor for Christian faith! - freedom and complete trust. I can think of other examples in life where freedom has proved so exhilarating, and I believe it applies to Christian faith too. For me, faith and grace have always been more important than external authority and law. When at the end of our morning worship I join with my congregation in saying:

From where we are, to where you need us
Jesus, now lead on.
From the security of what we know to the adventure of what you will show us
Jesus, now lead on.
To refashion this world until it resembles your kingdom
Jesus, now lead on.

- I mean it, and I want the opportunity to do it.

Let us look more closely at the way St Paul went about his mission – at a time today when the C of E is encouraging its churches to move 'from maintenance to mission.' Within about a decade before 57 AD Paul established churches in four provinces, then left quite confidently to travel out West to continue his work, as though he had completed the work where he had been. I suggest that today we would organise things differently:

stick around for a generation or so to check that everything was going well, people fully trained, teething problems dealt with, organisational supervision established. Despite the short time Paul spent at a particular church planting, he left them with the procedures and confidence to stand on their own feet in terms of choosing their ministers, celebrating the sacraments and knowing the traditions (however short). He also left each area to manage its own finances, without any instruction to send accounts for him to check.

'As the Lord has distributed to every man, as God has called each, so let them walk. ...... So ordain I in all the churches.'

Perhaps the word 'ordain' above simply means 'that was my way of working'. But Paul certainly did ordain ministers and left the church to work on its own difficulties and problems, with God as their guide. We don't do that – should we? We want to lay down an elaborate system of oversight, laws, traditions to follow, and forbid 'any form of service which is not authorised .....' Are we, by comparison with Paul's method, quenching the Spirit? When Paul has taught the basics, he says *'The rest will I set in order when I come.'* If his authority was resisted, he gave a democratic way to sort out the problem: *'at the mouth of two or three witnesses'*, 'though I admit he could lay down the law when this was justified. Mostly however he tries to give each congregation encouragement to sort out their own differences: for instance by encouraging good Christians to use their private influence to correct another member's fault. Sometimes the rebuke was quite gentle, such as the need to avoid their company.

Perhaps St Paul was trying deliberately to follow the example of Jesus himself. He too taught principles rather than laws. Not dictating to his disciples a rigid line of conduct, he told them to apply the general principles which should underpin their conduct and decision making.

St Paul had great confidence that the few churches he established in strategic places would become the centres of evangelism for that whole area. He told the Romans that he had *'fully preached the gospel of Christ from Jerusalem and round about ... '* - he trusted 'his' churches to get on with it even when he wasn't breathing down their necks – all the breath needed came from the Holy Spirit. His method showed huge reliance on and trust in God doing his own thing through the local congregation, who Paul treated with trust. They were trusted to *'give a reason for the hope that was in them'*.

This really was mission, not maintenance. They were given very elementary facts about the life and teaching of Jesus in the relatively short time Paul was with them, yet we read that tradesmen, slaves and old women knew how to give some account of God and did not believe without evidence.

Elsewhere in this book I write about my experience of the voluntary ministry (gained over more than forty years) and one aspect of this has to be the financing of ministry. St Paul goes to lengths to explain that his work for Christ does not put a financial burden on his churches. He is so anxious that his position should not be misunderstood that he mentions it many times. His practice seems to be that first, he did not seek any financial gain for himself. Second, he did not take finances to the churches he established - though there were some special cases of collecting money to carry for churches in need. Lastly, he did not administer church funds centrally.

In his time there were professional ministers, and Paul accepted that this was legitimate. He encouraged the church to make sure that those who worked were not out-of-pocket - his instruction not to muzzle the working ox as it trod the corn. But he thought that payment to him might reflect on the nature of his work and his motives, saying *'we bear all things that we cause no hindrance to the work of Christ'.* He added *'As a nurse cherishes her children, we were pleased to impart not only the gospel of God, but also our own souls, because you have become so very dear to us.' 'Remember our labour and travail, working night and day that we might not burden any of you, we preached to you the gospel of God.' 'We did not behave ourselves inappropriately among you, neither did we eat anyone's food without payment.'* In his last speech to the elders at Ephesus he stressed that he had made no money by his preaching and had supported himself by his own work: *'I envied nobody's money or clothes; you know that my own hands provided my needs.'*

It appears from Paul's letters that it was intended that each church (or area) should be financially independent, and have enough to support its workers and give to the poor. Our system takes money away from the people who give it, denying them the opportunity of charitable giving to known need, and gives a significant sum to central organisation. I know there's a problem here – ministers need to be trained, chaplains need to be paid, and so on – but is there another way?

In the same way that Jesus Christ revealed himself in the form of a servant, so the Christian churches were meant to serve their community financially and socially to meet local need. This was another way in which I think the early church was not institutionalised, centralised – it modelled a new way of life, Christ's way, the Servant King (*'hands that flung stars into space, to cruel nails surrendered'*). To appear servant-like is difficult if outsiders see lots of pomp and ceremony, apparent wealth and ornament in worship. I remember hearing a Bishop preach that Jesus did not wear fine robes and live in a palace: the Bishop said this whilst wearing fine robes and living in a palace, but did not seem to make the connection! From my experience of C of E organisation and worship I appreciate the beauty and in it see a reflection of the King of Kings; but to an outsider the event might suggest a quite different, negative thoughts.

I accept it's not that simple, but it is an area we need to think about. In one of my churches in a village of under 100 houses, I use an Elizabethan chalice which would no doubt fetch a lot of money at auction. But the beauty of that simple chalice is not in its price tag. It's in the fact that for several centuries those villagers have passed that same cup from mouth to mouth … *'the blood of Christ. Amen'* … and that is part of the mystery of the liturgy. We would lose a great deal by selling that chalice, even if it were allowed by the diocesan authorities (to whom it doesn't belong anyway but they would have to give permission!)

I am concerned about the way in which the finances of a local church get taken away from it, denying opportunity for its members to respond responsibly to people's need. A significant proportion of money given is syphoned off to the Diocese and taken away from those who gave it, much of the rest being eaten up by church fabric. The congregation at best do not understand this, and at worst think 'the church' is being greedy. The point is not whether such a perception is correct, but that it is common. To give an example.

As I write I have looked after a particular village church for over twenty years. The Diocese does not have to pay me, house me, pay towards pensions or Council Tax, etc.: the parishioners pay about £60 a week into diocesan funds but see no monies moving back to their local church. So they are bewildered why, when I take a funeral or a wedding, say, the Diocese requires what used to be called 'minister's fee' to be sent to the Diocesan Board of Finance who, after a while send most of it back to me. There are situations where the money returned does not cover my expenses for the event, so these have to be recovered from the PCC. It is an odd situation and difficult to justify – that I give my services free of charge yet both the PCC and myself have to pay money to the Diocese to allow me to do this. When a Diocese pays its priest, the congregation understands that such fees for occasional offices are useful in helping to meet the expenses of ministry – but when ministry is given without charge parishioners view the diocesan request as an unjustified demand which adds to their struggle to cope financially. It is another example of how some local churches, who are trying to be self-supporting, are crying out to be given more understanding, freedom and independence in their own affairs.

In my experience, and this is supported by wider research, the route via which most people come to faith in Jesus Christ is through other people – Word is still primarily expressed in flesh and blood. When I retired, instead of a special 'final service' we had a final party in the Village Hall. About one hundred folk turned up and between food, chatter and a little rock and roll they were invited to sign a book. I was moved by what they wrote: the remarks are interesting in that they make no mention of all the peripheral things that make media headlines during meetings of the Church government. All the remarks were about relationship, person to person. That is what they saw as the important thing I contributed.

Typical examples are: *'from our first day here you were so welcoming .... you were the one who fed me when I was unable to cook ..... I remember you bringing in two wet and drunken men who you had found stuck in a ford in a soft-top car: they were dried, fed, and went on their way .... you married us and baptised all our children .... your kindness, compassion and consideration made our union easy ...... so kind to me over the years ......you made the bell ringers giggle at weddings .....friendly manner and great good humour ....we enjoyed your company, your philosophy and even your jokes .... really appreciated your care, passion and wise words .... energy, commitment, enthusiasm and kindnesses ..... when I first told you of my situation you said that the church was not in the business of judging me .... the trauma of my wife's death was ameliorated tangibly by your tender and sensitive approach: she would have been so pleased that you accompanied her on her final journey .... thank you for being there for us in good times and in bad ...... for organising the community through my husband's heartbreaking illness and death and for helping him know that he was loved and supported to the last beat of his heart .... nothing is too much trouble, even rushing over to explain the TV won't work until you press the 'on' button! ..... thank you particularly for your help in my rather rocky faith journey ... we shall all miss your DIY in church ....you have been a figure of consistency and common sense, always finding the right word or mood for the occasion of village life ..... thank you for making a difference ... you are like our extended family and the father I never had ..... always been there for the key moments in my life ..... many years of love, friendship, shared memories, ups and downs ... we've had many adventures together ..... we really liked you coming to school and talking to us.'*

Now, all these comments are not written down to say *'Let us now praise famous men ...'* as in Ecclesiasticus chapter 44, because in a real sense they are not about me: they are about God. If, as a priest, I did not believe that I were a channel of communication for the Spirit of God, then I don't know what I was supposed to be! Any relationship which exhibits a measure of love, compassion, wisdom, understanding – this is a relationship in which God is speaking. In all the comments above there is no mention of God, yet they are all about God.

When people start their Christian pilgrimage they join a universal church but the door into it is local and personal. They join a local congregation which helps them to experience and grow a new life by walking together on the pilgrim path alongside others also growing in faith. But if new members are to be instrumental in sharing their new experience with others, the *'casting away of the former things'* cannot include a total breach with their old life. They live with the same family, do the same work, still pursue old leisure interests – and it is vital that they do, for that is their mission field. For them, this new life is expressed locally.

Certainly at first they have little need to know much about the national oversight given by the central organisation of their denomination. This is what I mean by their faith being obtained and lived out locally. Their feeling of responsibility and communion is with their fellows: the church they enter and the loyalty they express has a local address. We therefore need to be careful that the national administration and oversight appears to gently encourage and strongly support, rather than interfere by imposing rules and regulations. If the latter happens, then the hierarchy is no longer modelling the servant-hood of its founder. The national administration needs to be experienced at local level as the apex of an inverted pyramid, where the hierarchy are supporting the whole body, not applying pressure from above. I have no blueprint to revolutionise the hierarchy! - I'm just expressing how it often feels like in the local church. This ought not to be. We should find ways to give more freedom to local initiative and less feeling of control from 'he who must be obeyed'. How otherwise is the local church to become adult, mature?

Returning to the contrast shown by St Paul's way of working and oversight: he worked in such a way that his new churches soon stood on their own feet, not passively dependent on their founder. He could re-visit; he could write to them. But there was no intention of their remaining without responsibility for their own development. They were not designed to be in a situation where nothing could be done without authority and guidance from St Paul. With the freedom to act independently they were able to grow and learn from their own mistakes. The Holy Spirit was expected to guide them, so avoiding the possibility that they might put any person in the place of God. The various leaders in the church then had the opportunity to exercise their gifts. The C of E often depends too much on individual leadership and thrashes around like a headless chicken if its favourite leader should move on. Like children they mope around looking for a new daddy to look after them, tell them what to believe, what to do.

Writing this reminds me of one of the occasions when I was organising things during an interregnum. This happened in different church groups to which I was licensed and meant that I was the main continuity in those clusters for a total of more than six years. Every interregnum was fraught with difficulties and argument between different congregations. Not one went smoothly. In one group the disagreement was so great that the Diocese more or less made its own choice independent of the PCCs, and in my opinion it was a most inappropriate appointment. In my frustration following one particularly difficult meeting with representatives from all the parishes in the benefice, chaired by an Archdeacon and a Bishop (so organised because previously the Archdeacon alone had caused huge resentment by extraordinary mishandling of the group) I came home and wrote a sort of parable, which I now reproduce:

Once upon a time a father adopted four children and taught them how to live together as one family. The children had different personalities, different friends, different backgrounds, different interests – of course they'd had different fathers in their earlier years. But slowly they learned to live happily together. They shared many things, not least their stepfather who was wise enough to encourage them to keep their individuality. Some grew quite big and fairly independent; some were smaller and quite vulnerable. But under their father's care they got along together and appreciated the different contributions to the family which each made.

Then one day their stepfather went away. It was awful for them – like a death. Some grieved so much they became physically ill. Others went to look at the place where their stepfather had gone to live and work, even returning several times in the hope of seeing him again. Whilst they were missing him some outsiders asked 'What do you want most of all to replace your father?' Most people said 'We want our daddy back – or at least someone just like him. We want things to be like they were before.' It was a natural reaction.

But then some of the bigger ones began to realise that things could never go back to where they were. They had to accept the possibility that they might never have another father like their old one: perhaps this was an opportunity to start a new sort of life. So they went to the man who arranged new stepfathers and said 'Would it be possible to try a different way in the future?' Some of the other children were very upset indeed about this. 'Now you've made it impossible for us to have another daddy like our old one', they said.

This parable has a happy ending but I don't know what it is yet.

I copy this sad tale to illustrate how dependent on a

particular gifted priest congregation(s) become: how what we see as good leadership can in fact get in the way of churches being independently responsible and adult in their approach to running their own church. In family life the good parent is the one who is able to teach their children how to leave home: too often in church we keep our 'children' always dependent, never taking real responsibility for their own walk. It happens too when congregations have an inadequate priest – perhaps one simply not coping, not being the leader people expect, a poor preacher, one who is power-crazy – and I've worked with them all! Churches should not be so dependent on one leader and take so little responsibility for their own life in God. I was at one PCC meeting (in a church I did not lead) when I suggested that the PCC should work out a plan of mission in their village. One person said 'We don't do mission – that's what we pay the vicar for!' The tragedy was worsened by the fact that most of the others offered him support rather than embarrassment.

The experience of living through interregna, often repeated, makes me question why churches have to have an interregnum. I have heard all the arguments in favour, and none of them carry any weight with me. I know that the church is not a business in the usual sense of that word, but it does need to operate in a businesslike manner. No commercial enterprise would ever dream of leaving the organisation without a leader, often for a year or two. No church with which I have had contact has ever grown in number during an interregnum: rather, members have been lost particularly in the congregation where the previous incumbent lived. Every one.

Is that surprising? Most priests do not train and give our churchwardens or other officers experience of ministerial responsibility whilst there is a priest in office, and then we expect them to organise a congregation during an interregnum. I see much to be gained from changing the system so that as one priest leaves, another arrives. I write this one week from retirement, and as I walk round the village, people outside the normal congregation but very much part of my flock, ask one question more than any other, and it is this: 'Who has replaced you in the church?' When told that could take a year or more, they are astonished and ask 'Why?' So do I.

St Paul's churches had him around for about six months. Then he might go away and not visit again for eighteen months: they had been established and made self-reliant in one visit. If today we founded a church, ordained one of its members after six months and then left them to get on with the work, we would be thought mad! So, times have changed, but is there nothing to be learned from St Paul's confidence in his local congregations? Can we not trust that the local congregation knows more about how to best meet local needs (if it is allowed to retain its resources) than those who are foreign to this knowledge? Cannot the oversight be more supportive, less heavy in its touch?

Like St Paul, there is a need to keep in touch with individual churches and to offer advice when things go wrong. But there is a big difference between gentle, concerned oversight and imposing direct government. To repeat: Paul left his churches with basic knowledge of the life of Christ, the sacraments of Baptism and Eucharist and how to administer them, facts of important doctrine about such things as death and resurrection, and the Old Testament. They did not of course have the gospels. Perhaps it was the simplicity and brevity of this which made it so effective.

There were times where it all went wrong, as it did in Corinth with disgraceful conduct and immorality. But sin can be forgiven – that surely is central to the faith. If God is not in the business of forgiveness he isn't in business at all! I'm sure that the freedom they had been given, which allowed them to make mistakes, also gave a deeper sense of personal responsibility, a more real repentance, meaningful forgiveness and growth: there was no way they could blame anybody else. They had to realise they could not rely on St Paul to keep them out of mischief. They had to grow up.

By comparison we make our congregations accustomed to long-established and highly organised structures with lots of rules – only properly trained ministers may speak, only authorised services may be held, don't allow individual experiment, and so on. No wonder Christians are afraid to speak of their faith unless they have a qualification and written permission! We dare not take chances. St Paul baptised the jailer at Philippi on a simple confession of faith in Jesus – no long instructional programme there! I get the impression that if today St Paul heard the person saying *'come over to Macedonia; we need you here'*, that a voice from heaven (or is it the diocese) would say 'Don't you dare – you still have to get the counter-signature on your request to be given Permission To Officiate over there. Oh, and by the way, if you move don't you dare think of coming back to your old church for at least six months'.

I am asking the question: 'Would it be advantageous to encourage our church members, and particularly its leaders, to be less dependent on those who exercise authority over them, and more confident in making their own decisions about what is appropriate for their situation?' I believe a local leader should be ready to share real authority and ministry. As their priest we instruct, baptise, shepherd, take services and generally nurse them – just about everything. But what we are very reluctant to do is give them equality. If we are not careful we treat them as dependent 'dear children', still needing milk, but not as equals in the work of God. We who are priests must be very careful not to put ourselves in the place of Christ: does not the Holy Spirit who teaches us, inspire them too if we don't get in the way?

Confidence grows as people exercise their gifts. To constantly do things for people does not train them to be independent. A teacher has not failed when his pupil no longer needs his guidance: that's the very point when the instructor realises he has been successful. That's what teachers aim to do. We must resist telling people answers instead of letting them work through the problems by themselves. Some leaders will not step aside to give Christ elbow room: God no doubt stands behind metaphorically saying 'let my people free'! We should always ensure that our methods take seriously that God will enable those who have personal faith in him – I have seen Him give wings to the most unlikely members of the congregation!

It appears to me that one of the ways in which Paul

made his young churches self supporting was his way of choosing locally-grown leaders. He looked for people 'of good report' and put them in charge. The people knew their leader, were partly responsible for that choice and all the worshippers in each church had a certain responsibility to and for one another. The leaders were not sent away to be trained, later to be given a post in another place – the elders came from within the church to which they ministered, known to its members. This method encourages mutual responsibility. The leaders understood the difficulties and strengths of their own people and this seemed to Paul to be at least as important as the soundness of their theological knowledge or high intellect, though it was essential that they had high morals. I am intrigued by Paul's instruction *'If it be possible let him (the Bishop) be a teacher, but if he be illiterate, let him be persuasive and wise in speech; let him be advanced in years.'* That sounds strange to the way we organise things.

Some appear to have been appointed to perform sacraments, who were not what we now call priests – and these were held in high respect. These people also could ordain others. Unlike our own situation, Paul ordained several elders in the same church, so everything was not dependent on or concentrated in one person. Contrast this to a priest today in a small rural situation where he/she is preacher, teacher, administrator, architect/builder/fundraiser, verger, secretary, ... oh, and priest! But then again we were taken away for a few years to be expensively trained and examined! We say that the sharing of bread and wine is of first importance between Christians and the only 'service' which Christ commanded to be done in memory of him. Does it really require great education and training to do this? Yet we seem to put intellectual qualifications and enabling pieces of paper ahead of a starving congregation.

Our intellectual requirement can also mean that those ordained are out of touch with the very people they come to serve. In the past it was normal for the dimmer son to enter the priesthood rather than, say the military. Later it was common for the path to be Private School, Public School, Oxbridge, Theological College, then go into a parish and be relevant! That is difficult even for the most gifted. Happily we are leaving that behind, but I believe we are far too cautious in the way we appoint our priests.

Can it not happen that the natural person to lead a congregation is someone who is a leader in the parish already? If not, the church loses its prophets, and the prophets lose their opportunity to exercise their gifts.

With basic training and continued support, such people would make excellent church 'elders'. But we lack both the faith (guts?) to act in that way, and we have not developed the vehicle to deliver support and encouragement needed to operate that way. We supply a church with a stranger for its leader, wrap him/her in red tape, and offer what (from the receiving end) often feels more like oversight than encouragement, from a system which seems remote.

Chapter Nine

The History of the Volunteer Ministry.

I greatly dislike the title of Non Stipendiary Minister, and was once careless enough to suggest to a Bishop that he could call me a Non Stipendiary Minister if I could call him a Hireling Bishop. But I shall take a deep breath and use 'NSM' to mean all those who do not receive a stipend in return for their ministry, whether in the workplace or parish church. In reality it is difficult to be prescriptive in describing the typical NSM, because we are pretty well unique when it comes to individual mission. Some are parish based (and not unlike a traditional stipendiary), some workplace focussed (taking the initiative in developing a unique expression of their calling) and some, like myself, are both. Elsewhere I have reflected on what it has been like for me over four decades, and what there is to learn from that experience.

All priests are fishermen/women but we do our fishing in different waters, using different techniques. There is a communication between NSMs working within the M25, and one of its members Richard Spence makes an interesting point about 'fishing for men.' Simon Peter fished with nets and that's one way of capturing people and holding them until they reach land. Some use a lure to attract (an analogy might be the promise of eternal salvation if they get caught). Yet others in the church make the equivalent of an attractive lobster pot with inviting things on offer inside, and wait for the fish to arrive. But the NSM takes to scuba diving, entering the fishes' own world to share their experience of God. You can now see where my book title 'Swimming With the Fishes' comes from.

I have already memtioned my experience. my credentials. An NSM for over four decades, working in a parish or group of parishes. When in work I developed a special ministry which was extra-parochial, frequently crossing parish, deanery and Diocesan boundaries. In a parish setting I have been effectively in charge of one or more parishes, never taking less than sixty services a year. I have led/organised interregna (it's often the NSMs who provide the continuity at such times) and have worked through an additional five years of what was legally a vacancy. That means I was without local senior oversight or support for eleven years in total. In February 2012 I retired with Permission To Officiate.

Having this experience (bias?) it's not surprising that I see Jesus as an NSM. I wonder if you are familiar with this poem by G A Studdert-Kennedy.............

The Carpenter

I wonder what he charged for chairs at Nazareth.
And did men try to beat him down
And boast about it in the town-
"I bought it cheap for half-a-crown
From that mad Carpenter?"
And did they promise and not pay,
Put it off to another day;
O, did they break his heart that way,
My Lord, the Carpenter?
I wonder did he have bad debts,
And did he know my fears and frets?
The gospel writer here forgets
To tell about the Carpenter.
But that's just what I want to know.
Ah! Christ in glory, here below
Men cheat and lie to one another so;
It's hard to be a carpenter.

I've sometimes wondered if Jesus was ever asked to make crosses for the occupying power. Then there was the NSM Peter, who continued his fishing whilst Jesus was around. Add to these the tent maker – elsewhere in this book I have illustrated how Paul went to great lengths to make sure that whilst he was establishing churches he was always self-supporting, paying his own way. Yes, I think I could make a case for there being NSMs from the beginning.

Church History however has little place for ordained ministers who are not 'full-time' - a ridiculous phrase, as if it is ever possible to be a part-time priest, given that a priest is something which you are, not something which you do. Within the last 200 years however lone voices have asked the question 'Why Not?' Within the last 200 years such voices have been ignored by the establishment. The following notes owe much to a Paper written recently by Barry Wilson entitled 'Non-Stipendiary Ministry: From Radical Idea to New Beginning', found on-line.

The headmaster of Rugby School in 1841 was Thomas Arnold. He was deeply concerned that the parish priest had completely lost touch with the working classes in industrial areas. He suggested that bridges could be built if men who worked could also be ordained, so as to touch the lives of ordinary people. W H Hale, the Archdeacon of London, brought the proposition to convocation on several occasions. One obstacle to be overcome was the Pluralities Act which made it impossible for a clergyman to hold another profession. A Bill to overturn this 'Deacon's (church of England) Bill' was eventually formulated but it failed because clergy were not willing to compromise their professional status.

The reasons for opposing the priest-worker idea can be said to be selfish rather than theological, and it would not be the last time that clergy have proved to be very conservative when it comes to challenging their status quo – it is still happening. In mid-Victorian times clergy had seen their status rise to that of 'gentleman', whereas a century earlier many were viewed as lacking in education, rustic, of poor lifestyle.

So the defeat of the Deacon's Bill meant that interest in NSMs declined until another crisis arose. After the First World War there were too few ordinands to keep the Ship of Fools afloat. The Diocesan Conference in London and Southwark asked people to examine the theological reasons for not allowing clergy to have secular employment. When discussed fully in 1925 you can guess the result – it was inconclusive! Again the drive towards such a movement was lost. Along came Ronald Allen, sometimes called the prophet of Non-stipendiary ministry, a missionary in China with the USPG. He suggested not only that the leadership, authority and structures in the C of E were against the will of God and unscriptural, but they ignored a whole pool of lay talent wanting to be tapped. In 1923 he had published 'Voluntary Clergy' which gave strong arguments promoting the idea of what we now call NSMs. For years he wrote to the press, published articles and corresponded with the church hierarchy. Nothing happened.

The idea was first picked up overseas and then came to the Lambeth Conference of 1930 for which Allen had published a paper 'The Case for Voluntary Clergy'. The Conference was unable to support the measure, maybe because it looked as if the number of ordinands was beginning to rise again: a case of forget the theology, we may not need this newfangled idea. There was class-driven snobbery amongst the clergy who thought that joining with working men might lower the tone. But there were chinks in the armour. The Conference acknowledged there was *no insuperable objection .....* *under proper safeguards .... where the need is great.'* Then more inertia.

In 1935 F R Barry again promoted the idea of voluntary ministry in his book 'The Relevance of the church.' (Note: thank you Amazon on line! However old or niche a book may be, it's likely that someone somewhere has it for sale. Some of the volumes I have purchased via that route to research this book are so little sought after that I have been charged £0.01 plus postage!) Barry considered that paid ministers were by their very nature trained to safeguard against contamination of the church by the world. Therefore the system produced a clerical caste which drove a wedge between the church and daily life. Barry suggested that a volunteer minister within the workplace would demonstrate that such a division was false – all church members were potential ministers. Stipendiary clergy did not like the idea, so the church had to wait another twenty years, including another world war.

After the War the church had to take notice that the number of paid clergy had been in decline for decades, together with the numbers of infant baptisms, confirmations and Easter communicants. Again the church was playing the numbers game rather than employing theology to suggest the need to look again at voluntary ministry. There was still no real enthusiasm for such a change. Some people kept the idea alive, one of whom was the person who ordained me in Southwark Cathedral in 1971. This was Mervyn Stockwood who chaired a sub-committee of a church Assembly Report 'Towards the Conversion of England' in 1945. One recommendation was:

'In some circumstances a parish priest should be allowed to take a job in industry for a shorter or longer

period. In exceptional circumstances, an industrial worker should be ordained as a deacon or priest, to remain in industry and exercise his ministry as an industrial worker.'

So, a small chink in the clericalised armour, but only *'In exceptional circumstances'*! The idea was being given a chance in South Yorkshire in 1944. Ordinands were encouraged to work for a while in a Sheffield factory. But more than that: a man who wanted to continue in the factory as a paid worker could be ordained.

While imprisoned in 1944 Dietrich Bonhoeffer had written:

'The church is the church only when it exists for others. To make a start it should give away all its property to those in need. The clergy must live solely on the free will offerings of their congregations or possibly engage in some secular calling.'

Revolutionary stuff indeed – 'though of course he was a Lutheran!

So by 1955 a permanent change in the law was under discussion, to allow the secular employment of clergy which had been prohibited by the old Pluralities

Act. It had not gone without notice that in any case some clergy were illegally supporting their income by moonlighting in a paid job! The reasoning of that time was first, that volunteer ministers would fill the numbers gap - where have I heard that before?: it's still advanced by some as to why NSMs are a good idea only when they support 'proper' priests! Secondly, people with pastoral responsibility (in welfare, youth work, doctors, etc.) and people in industry might be ordained, rather like a school chaplain might be ordained and teach. In 1958 Barry's arguments were influential with the 'Committee on Supplementary Ministry' which suggested:

'in view of competent theologians there is no theological principle which forbids a suitable man from being ordained a priest while continuing in secular occupation.'

They recommended that the Lambeth Conference should give its *'cautious backing'* to the idea with the resolution *'The Conference now wishes to go further and to encourage provinces to make provision along these lines.'*

There was still huge reluctance, even opposition to such ministry from clergy who thought their status would be undermined. Again the numbers game surfaced with people saying that voluntary clergy were not needed any more because due to the evangelistic efforts of the likes of Billy Graham, numbers and finances in the C of E were healthier. However after the idea had been discussed in Convocation (three times!) the Canon Law was revised. In 1964, only four years before my calling, the 'Clergy (Ordination and Miscellaneous Provisions) Measure' – a catchy title! - removed legal constraints to non stipendiary ministry. So a question asked in 1841 was finally given a firm answer after one hundred and twenty three years! However individual Bishops had discretion in adopting this revolution, which has often been the situation subsequently when seeking majority agreement concerning changes in C of E practice.

So it was that 'my' two Bishops at the time, Mervyn Stockwood and John Robinson took a unilateral decision to establish the Southwark Ordination Course. Mervyn Stockwood was controversial, an innovator and enabler who put together a course which became a blueprint for the C of E. There are many anecdotes about Mervyn (and I have a few of my own!) but one will suffice to show that he was prepared to be rebellious. On the eve of a General Synod in York his chaplain presented him with the relevant documents – all five hundred and one pages. Mervyn said *'Now, I am going to do something that will shock you'*, and threw the lot into the waste-paper basket. He then said *'You are looking at the freest man in the Church of England.'* In retrospect, every single ordained minister who has been a role model for me has been a significant rebel, willing to bend the rules and innovate. When the late Steve Jobs was CEO of Apple computers, one of their commercials said *'The people who are crazy enough to think they can change the world are the ones who do.'* Mervyn was such a person.

As early as June 1979 he had stated that he had plans to establish a new form of training for the ministry. A year earlier from the pulpit he had said:

'I think it is likely that in addition to the parochial system we need a more flexible type of church organisation and that in addition to the parochial priesthood we need an order of worker priests – men who will stay on the ground floor, earning their living as factory hands, bus drivers, railwaymen, trades union officials, shopkeepers and schoolmasters. And as they go about their daily jobs it will be their duty to act as Christian propagandists and to build up the church.'

It was not a new idea for him. As early as 1943 Archbishop William Temple had written to Mervyn:

'I think it may be a very good thing that some clergy

should be working in ordinary jobs, still carrying on spiritual ministrations as they have opportunity; but economically dependent on their secular job.'

The Southwark Ordination Course was designed *'to train men from a wide experience and background with no age limit and open to men wishing to serve a full-time parochial ministry and to men who want to engage in some form of supplementary ministry.'* The reader should note that when Mervyn said 'men' he meant 'men and women' because the training course contained both sexes. The first students were ordained by Mervyn at Michaelmas 1963. The SOC opened with sixty three applicants and half were accepted. By 1980 two hundred had been ordained, half of them non stipendiaries.

I think that, perhaps for the first time in many generations, people were able to consider that voluntary ministry could possibly be much more than just an expedient for supporting the parochial ministry at a time of insufficient stipendiary priests. This realisation is still yet to dawn in some minds fifty years later, that natural leaders in congregations can be priests in their own work, as teachers, doctors, factory workers and in other so-called secular situations. Perhaps because the hierarchy has not yet appreciated the new movement, it has not made much effort to change systems of discipline, administration and support for volunteer ministers. I recently asked the leaders of a diocese which already has more NSMs in licence than stipendiaries, if they had knowledge of what 'their' volunteer ministers did when they were not in a parish setting. I was told they had no idea: they had never asked the question! A huge amount of ministry is taking place to which the hierarchy, by default, is blind. They seem unwilling to conceive of ordained ministry other than that of the parish priest, except for a small number of chaplains in prison, hospitals, etc.

In the past the priest knew his place, and that place was in and around the parish church. There are many dangers to this blinkered existence, not least an unwelcome departmentalism and narrowing of the priestly role by which some parish priests become limited to liturgical, ecclesiological and other specialist interests, isolated from the life of the world. A volunteer priest with ministry outside the parish(es) to which (s)he is licensed is demonstrating that there is indeed an essential ministry of all believers embracing all life. There are priests in the wider community safeguarding against clerical dominance in one profession. Is not this a return to apostolic practice? It also offers to the church priests who are mature, experienced and competent in a secular role. It is arguably asking too much of a person in their early twenties to travel the route of public school, Oxbridge and Theological College to then go into a parish and 'fit in' usefully.

The Body of Christ, like all bodies, is not fixed: it is alive and developing, or rather it will develop if it really is alive. Just as the physical body is constantly exchanging it's very atoms with the environment (for atoms cannot normally be created or destroyed), so the spiritual body needs to change. This is a sign of life itself – the incorporation of new forms, never finished, always developing, never a static institution. In his own words, God *is making a new thing'* if we let him! I like to think that the emergence again of a volunteer priesthood is a sign of life in addition to being a threat to the status quo!

I trained from 1968 to 1971, part of a group of over 30 ordinands Some were not Anglican and others could not at that stage be ordained because they were women. For instance I shared time on SOC with Dr. Una Kroll who, when Synod voted against the ordination of women uttered those famous words *'we asked for bread, and you have offered us a stone.'* Two evenings a week lectures took place in London under the auspices of the University of London. We also spent many weekends each year (for over three years) in residence at

Wychcroft, the Southwark Diocesan training house, and also had two week Summer Schools as part of our training.

It was rigorous and tough for those of us in fulltime occupation, and difficult on family life. But the training, identical for those called to stipendiary and non stipendiary positions, was excellent. It allowed working people who had neither the money nor the public school education to consider ordination training, and also attracted lively candidates considered too old for stipendiary ministry. Some of us, certainly myself, felt a definite calling to the non stipendiary ministry, and whilst I have subsequently been offered a stipendiary post in the past on more than one occasion, that was not for me ('though many others did take up that option and I wonder how many of my fellow students stayed non stipendiary for over four decades, as I did.)

In April 2002 in an article 'Ministers at Work' Davis Fisher wrote *The presence of the ordained tent-maker invites faith based dialogue in a neutral setting, especially with people who are not church-goers'* and in the same article he quoted the late Archbishop Michael Ramsay (who came on a couple of occasions to our training weekends in the 1960s): *'I regard the contemporary development of a priesthood which combines a ministry of word and sacrament with employment in a secular profession not as a modern fad but as a recovery of something indubitably apostolic and primitive. This is to say that what we call our tent-makers today belong most truly to the apostolic foundation, and we may learn from them of that inward meaning of priesthood which we share with Jesus Christ.'*

A brief story as an aside. One weekend during our training Archbishop Michael Ramsay turned up in his chauffeur driven Morris Minor; it was a session when we were acting out a baptism with dolls. A colleague said jokingly *'what happens if you drop the baby in the font?'* Quick as a flash the Archbishop replied *'Put on the lid and continue with the service for a burial at sea'!* I always thought that the good Archbishop, whose physical appearance suggested that he was on his last legs, had a mind as sharp as a razor!

The 'tent-making' minister was by then appearing in numbers in some (but not all) dioceses. Dr Forrest Lowry stated in 2003 *''Tent-making' in God's eyes is ministry .... We all need to remember that God called every believer to full-time Christian service. Every believer is called to minister .... There is no 'secular' or 'spiritual' dimension in God's vocabulary.'*

There is a paragraph in 'Being a Priest Today', by C Cocksworth and R Brown: *'Our calling to build up the life of the church is not an excuse to distance ourselves from the life of the world. In fact, it should propel us into the world so that we can model the priestly attention to the world which is the calling of all Christians as they serve the Christ who gave himself up for all.'*

So the movement which made it possible for candidates to train for all types of ministry side-by-side had begun, and spread to other centres. I find it interesting that despite almost fifty years of NSMs (of various calling) entering the church as ordained ministers, even today there can be resistance, misunderstanding and prejudice expressed towards such ministry from stipendiary clergy at both local and diocesan level. This will be made more evident in the section in which I share the findings of a number of recent surveys of the profession, and also when I tell of my first-hand experience of being a volunteer minister.

I am convinced that it is not acceptable just to assume that people will come to church – we must go to them. To be effective we have to plant the sacred within the secular, which is what NSMs try to do in their ministry. In doing this we tread a lonely path as pioneers, whilst at the same time being aware that such ministry is apostolic and prophetic. We are 'singing a new song' which has not been heard for far too long. A church which is committed to being the body of Christ is fundamentally incarnational: I believe NSMs have many more opportunities to demonstrate that to Joe Public than some other models of priesthood, because of their different social and professional setting. NSMs are not to be ignored, and it might be salutary to mention that we have been available for almost fifty years in this very conservative church of ours, and a Google search for 'NSM priest' now turns up over 1.5 million references!

Chapter Ten

NSM Ministry – a Rationale

In this section I do not wish to denigrate in any way the vast majority of stipendiary priests who do a wonderful job for the church. For instance when a village church is the only surviving place where people can meet, where 'our vicar' is a profound leader of village life, it works very well. But to fulfil its purpose more fully the church as a whole needs to change. I want to suggest that there is a growing well of fellow workers who are called to a different shape of ministry. We should look at the rationale of their situation. Today fewer and fewer stipendiaries struggle with the cure of more and more souls. But I am not promoting non-stipendiaries as those who fill the gaps only. I want to advance the thought that the church has lost its way, has ignored the sense of what it is for, how it could work more effectively.

The need for the good news of Jesus is as evident as ever. Although there are real enemies to the gospel there are also the seekers, the half believing, the wistful. Not all non church goers are the enemies of Christ. The Anglican church is available and, at its best, its borders are open. Much of our evangelism is in the context of pastoral care: within the parish context there is no sharp divide between preaching the gospel and shepherding souls. But to continue with that image, sheep do not heed the voice of strangers. Evangelism is never more effective than when it is not just left to 'experts', but when ordinary Christians share their faith. I think what I want to emphasise is that evangelism happens in the world because that is where God chooses to be, incarnated. Evangelism is not about getting people into church, it is about Christians being in the world where people are, where God is, and inviting them into the Kingdom.

Christianity began as a lay movement. Jesus could have chosen the professionals – scribes, Pharisees, Sadducees, Levites – to be his fellow workers, but he didn't. The ordained ministry as we know it was not instituted by Christ pesonally and the distinction between laity and clergy did not become apparent for a long time. But after it did appear, the clericalisation was rapid and often rigid. The Bible picture of the priesthood of all believers appears to me to suggest that the main work of the ordained priesthood is to enable the priesthood of all Christians, so that they may present God to their neighbours. In some situations today however it appears that there are priests who disable the laity and keep them in a state of dependence.

As I wrote earlier, a church in decline which has no idea how to tackle the majority is in serious trouble. Yet it often appears to be obsessed with saving itself rather than the world. Can it learn afresh how to be Jesus in the world? We need to realise that the church is a means to an end: it is where the labourers meet for refreshment, fellowship and teaching before they return to their real work of healing, teaching, feeding, outside the church building.

Jesus cannot be imposed on people: transformation of life happens when people become captivated and intrigued by the Saviour, usually glimpsed in the life of a neighbour. He suggested that the Kingdom was a bit like finding treasure by accident, and certainly not like being hit around the head with a plank! Paul's advice to Christians in a town where he had to escape to avoid a riot was *'make it your ambition to lead a quiet life, to mind your own business and to work with your hands ... so that your daily life may win the respect of outsiders'.*

So the Tentmaker advises in the widest sense that we should *'work with our hands'* within society. The author Ruth Etchells, discussing a shift of the church into mission-mode twenty years ago, had this to say:

'what readers, non-stipendiary clergy, lay preachers

and other similar callings – in their various forms throughout the church can offer is so special that one longs to see the institutional church glorying more in this gift from God .... For the glory of these people is that they belong equally in the secular world and in the institutional church, in a way no one else does. All of them have been publicly commissioned and accredited to certain liturgical and pastoral functions in the church: but on the strict understanding that they keep also their secular identity as workers in the world and in business or education or industry or whatever. As such, they are able to interpret the two areas of God's action to each other. So it is vital that their non-churchy insights should be emphasised and called on in all thinking about structures, training and worship in the church and the church's missionary activity in the world. They are some of the key members of the institutional team where secular context should never be threatened or whittled away in favour of their 'churchy' identity. They should be delighted in, honoured and used! As one of God's special mercies to his community of believers.'

Speaking from my own experience of such ministry, I must say that some of those who have had oversight of me over the years has not agreed with what Ms Etchells has to say. With regard to her penultimate sentence I have been offered (and refused) stipendiary posts which have been offered as a more real, a better way of doing ministry. When I come later in this study to share the response to recent surveys of NSMs it is evident that such ministers feel ignored, uncherished, underused.

Early in the first book of our Bible we learn that part of God's purpose for his children is to work: to care for and exercise dominion over His Creation, to till the ground and keep the garden. Work is not a curse, it is part of being humans made in the image of God and stewards of His Creation. I am told that the Hebrew word for work is the same as the word for worship. If we think of work as 'service', suddenly the word takes on a new theological dimension. Work becomes part of the everything we do *'to the glory of God'*. In his letter to the Colossian Christians St Paul urges *'Whatever you do, work at it with all your heart, as working for the Lord, not for men.'* I am not here making a case to say that being a stipendiary minister is not 'work' – we all know it is very hard work! - I am saying that other work is not inferior, of less value. If God's intention is that we should work then it isn't a bad idea to have a trained minister to help interpret what God is doing there. Experience is that work colleagues treat an NSM with interest and respect, other Christians in the workplace welcome your status with joy, and may even become a little bolder in their own faith expression. However it is fair to say that it is not always easy to get the right balance between ministry at work and back home in the parish where they might view you as a freebie and gobble you up if you do not keep control over it.

Christian ministers at work need to remember that God wants them not as a reflection of someone else: each has a unique ministry which to a large degree will be shaped by them and God and nobody else. There is not for the NSM the security of a parochial ministry blueprint. There will be perhaps no precedent for the pattern of service they develop. The NSM is often flying by the seat of their pants, fingers crossed that God will rescue them when they get into trouble. Some call that faith! What the minister discovers is that if you place yourself unconditionally in God's wind of change, then quite simply things happen: things you'd never dream of. It's not the dog collar which creates opportunity, or the long black garb of another age ('salvation through haberdashery') - it is God.

So nobody should be surprised when God makes something happen in the workplace through the work of a minister there. I am reminded of the story of a man who took his wife to watch her first cricket match. The crowd exploded in applause when a fielder made a great catch, but the wife said 'I thought that is what he was there for'! Exactly. The minister is where (s)he is to be used by God. Many non churchgoers find 'preach' a perjorative term and have no respect for someone with whom they do not have a high degree of trust and identification. The NSM is not detached in that way – (s)he can influence hearts and actions as a caring, loving colleague with a vulnerable capacity for self disclosure.

Here is an illustration – not typical I am pleased to say - of how detached a stipendiary can become if they lose touch with the real world outside church: the sort who has been told that to have friends inside the parish is anathema. A missionary returned to the UK from abroad. He said that his local church kept him at a distance. Wanting a lift to a Diocesan Synod he rang his parish priest to ask for a lift. The parish Secretary responded with 'The rector does not give lifts to people.'

I live near a town to which many vicars retire. Having been told not to make friends in their old parish, they have left with the instruction not to return there for six months. The effect is very cruel, their first year particularly so. There is often illness because of the inability to adapt, and wives are badly affected (most of the retirees at this time being male). The Clergy Training

Officer of a York Archdeaconry asked in a newspaper article if 'friendship and priesthood were ever compatible': his answer was that they are not! How extraordinary to think that an element of detachment and objectivity is incompatible with friendship! I can think of someone who had no problem with choosing twelve very dear friends to share ministry, some of which very specially close. We can't be fully human (or even sane!) without friends to share every day with.

A church which is not taking seriously what God is doing in the world is a positive hindrance. A church which seems to stay in a locked stone box appears to say nothing about the world outside, which sees it as a massive irrelevance. In the world of work people think they have permission to do what they like because God never goes there! Unless the church gets more involved with people where they spend their life, it will be seen as an incomprehensible survival from the past, scratching where people do not itch any more.

The Bible asks 'How shall they hear without a preacher?' The Christian at work is that preacher, and the ordained worker can be very well equipped to interpret God to people. I think it was Archbishop Rowan Williams who said that the church is what happens when man responds to what God is doing in his world. I was once lunching with a previous Archbishop, the late Robert Runcie, when he told me of an MP who stood up to object to what a colleague had said in Parliament with the admonition 'Hands off the church of England: it is the only thing which stands between us and Christianity'!

A move towards encouraging a priestly presence in the workplace will deploy the church's resources in the most appropriate place, where people are now rather than where they were in the Middle Ages. Being God in the world is about identification: it is about speaking the language of God in flesh and blood. But to repeat, for the NSM there might be little security of routine in their witness, little pattern to follow. Each has to listen to God and work out the shape of their own pilgrim path as a minister. It requires huge confidence in God's providence. Each moment consists in doing what is appropriate in this new situation as you take Christ to where people are, living and earning in the political, social, educational and economic world of work. The NSM is the sacramental person in that workplace, an oasis in a secular desert. If you are willing to be the salt of the earth, adding flavour and stopping corruption, you have to be ready to be rubbed into people's wounds. Leavening the lump requires being well mixed into it if you are to be a person of hope in a world of despair.

The worker priest will reach thousands of people who never enter a church building. When teaching thousands of teenagers there was hardly any problem which did not come my way or blessing I was not privileged to share. It is just a case of taking seriously what God is doing in the world and responding to Him there: showing there is another way (which someone once cleverly said involves disturbing the comfortable and comforting the disturbed). Christ was successful partly because he got down and dirty. He did not sit in an office communicating with imaginary friends on Facebook. He challenged people where they were, threw market stalls about. In the cruel and crude world into which Jesus was born the Kingdom began not in world shattering headlines, but in a meeting between God and His people at their level – and it still is.

For those who think they have rejected the institutional church or are scared at crossing its threshold, the worker priest offers a new avenue to explore a relationship with God. The non churched have an opportunity to observe, listen and debate with a minister in the ordinary world. A surprising number are hungry for meaning and a spiritual dimension in their lives, yet are unlikely to 'go to church' in their search. If they do go to church they might feel that they have immediately been un-churched because every service is Holy Communion, only for the Confirmed. Or they might go to a church addicted to a Family Service which is so simple that it encourages them to remain spiritual babies. A similar result (lack of maturity) will be achieved if the resident priest has a habit of substituting for the sermon a simple, short 'word for the day'. John Stott wrote 'sermonettes produce Christianettes.' Some priests are fiercely territorial and this too can be a problem to welcoming newcomers. People don't want to be told rules they must obey in order to be accepted: Edward Schillebeeckx said we need 'a church with a more human face.'

Jesus expanded the priesthood to include all Christian believers, male and female, but did train some who he chose as special leaders. It has been said that the job of a worker priest is to discover God in the workplace and to serve him there. The point of course is that God got there first. The church (partly expressed in ordained non stipendiary ministers) needs to put its head above ecclesiastical trenches and build bridges of relationship in society. Any functioning bridge has to be properly grounded at both ends to be any good. This would be a sign that God takes people's everyday lives seriously and that the church commits its ambassadors to share the lives of those it seeks to serve.

Jesus had a problem of getting away from people rather than getting them to come and hear him. Why? - because he spoke differently to the religious elite around him. His message was the best thing they had heard. They found him revolutionary – 'the common people heard him gladly'. He should not now be represented by one of the most conservative institutions on the planet where the main teaching is more a monologue than dialogue.

Chapter Eleven

Fifty Years On, How Are NSMs Received?

I have been anxious to confirm, largely from my own experience, that the ministry of an NSM can be fulfilling and exciting for the minister and readily used by the people. I do not believe that to be in doubt. But as far as the C of E organisation is concerned, NSMs are invisible unless they plunge into traditional parish ministry. This chapter shares typical surveys of NSMs which have been conducted recently. It does not make easy reading.

The church Times made a big thing of reporting one such survey in the Spring of 2011 under the headline 'Unpaid, disregarded and underused'. Teresa Morgan asked NSMs how they were treated in the church. At that time NSMs formed 27% of all clergy – the number is now greater – and she described their 'vigorous' views as 'from the comic to the shocking'. Over a year earlier she had suggested that there should be a national survey to establish what such ministers do, as a basis for planning: none had appeared, so she did it herself as a web-based survey. She rang all sixty seven UK diocesan offices to find that no national list of NSMs existed. Only twenty five dioceses had an NSM officer, and one such post was shared by two particular dioceses but only one was aware of it! Only three dioceses knew instantly that they had such an officer and what their name was. Nevertheless a survey was undertaken and of the NSMs contacted, about nine hundred took part in the survey.

Happily, she found that stipendiaries and non stipendiaries were, on the whole, trained side by side, and after ordination almost 100% of unpaid priests had over a year of continuing ministerial development. Most dioceses made training available to NSMs by scheduling all training out of normal working hours, but not all. One respondent was sent ministerial review times by her Archdeacon, all in working hours. She asked for other times but never heard from the Archdeacon again! In summary, there is some way to go before NSMs are properly integrated into diocesan and deanery structures and provisions.

Of the respondents, 71% assisted in parish ministry, and 13% were responsible for their parish or similar (as I always was). 41% had no change in their ministry since ordination, only 14% having gained additional responsibilities. Of those involved in parish ministry only 12.5% had changed parishes. Some had lost responsibility when a new stipendiary prevented them from continuing as previously. Incidentally, people viewed the lack of movement not as stability, but as stagnation. One sentence of the report is this: *'Far too often, it seems, dioceses train ordinands at considerable expense, ordain them, place them in a parish or chaplaincy, and then just forget about them.'*

Perhaps it is more sad that many NSMs felt they had been badly treated by stipendiaries, particularly their incumbents. Often this was due to having a new incumbent following a time of rewarding ministry with a previous one. Some NSMs found they were denied the opportunity to preach for years on end, or to take services. Sometimes they were not allowed any pastoral position, not kept informed of events, not allowed to develop initiatives. One NSM asked 'Why did God bother to call me if I wasn't going to be used?' Sometimes Bishops were helpful in such cases, sometimes their advice amounted to praying about it, but no respondent reported a case where the Bishop or Archdeacon had taken up the problem effectively with the stipendiary.

Some stipendiaries had said they felt threatened because their NSM was a more experienced priest than they were or held a senior job in secular life. The main problem however was that too many stipendiaries viewed NSMs as less important, amateurs not to be trusted. It is not unknown for a stipendiary to ask 'Are you a proper priest or an NSM?' Misunderstandings are evident in questions such as 'Why do you need to be ordained if you are not working for the church?', or 'How do you find time to be a priest with all the other things you do?' Almost all those who answered the survey had at some time been made to feel second class – weekenders, hobby priests. They felt they were viewed as disproportionately old, unable to give enough time to the church to be useful, lacking in leadership and not deployable. The survey showed that none of these situations were factual. For instance, more than a quarter were already giving over 30 hours a week to their ministry (almost half over 20 hours).

The happiest stories came from those who had created their own unique package of work ministry and/or been in charge of a parish – so no wonder I have been doubly happy! It was noted that in terms of leadership material the majority of NSMs had held down a paid job – banking, teaching, medicine, the armed forces, accountancy, civil servants, law, scientific work and business. Many were leaders in their professions but in addition had extensive experience of church life having done things like church planting, fund raising, teaching, leading retreats and pilgrimages, organising music, administration. A substantial majority had led

---

Michael Johnson

interregna, frequently two years or more long. Some commented wryly that the diocese was happy to leave them to run things when an incumbent left but treated them as 'not leadership material' when a new stipendiary was appointed.

A very sad finding of the survey is that many NSMs felt they had no significant ministry outside the parish. There should be some diocesan support and encouragement to help them with that. Those who had developed a ministry at work demonstrated that the nature of this varied widely: I do not find this surprising. But for those who have no such ministry, it is a hugely wasted opportunity for the church which does not help them to be missionaries in society. Training seems to ignore this and certainly none of the hierarchy have ever asked me details about what I do outside of the parishes to which I am licensed. One respondent wrote *'Selection was a nightmare. The selectors did not understand MSE. Weird really, as professional colleagues understood it straight away and were fully supportive.'* If the church is a serious about mission as it proclaims, it needs to work on this.

The author comments that the response to her survey however was far from grumpy. People spoke much of privilege and joy as they worked out their

172

vocation, but were bitter that their diocese seemed to ignore their offer of gifts, time and expertise. They said things like *'My experience is that Human Resource issues are badly handled'; 'Structures of support, accountability and challenge are either non existent or astonishingly bad'; 'I have been disappointed to discover the extent to which the church of England is reluctant to admit to the gifts that mature SSMs can bring to their ministry from their professional backgrounds.'*

Following those articles in the church Times, readers sent in a number of letters. Here's what some said:

'I undertook two years research. I received 80 contributions from all over England, and the findings were almost identical to those in Dr Morgan's article. Words like invisible, not counted, overlooked, marginalised were very common. One incumbent told his NSM that he did not delegate to him because people might not like their baptisms, weddings and funerals done by a mere NSM. Some were bullied and told they had no authority, by churchwardens.'

In other places NSMs having read Dr Morgan's report, responded with comments (from different sources) such as:

'The church of England treats its ministers appallingly – it is in and of the culture – systemic. The Bishops couldn't care less: the pastoral care ranges from abysmal to non-existent. It is confusing to introduce the term SSM in this context when in current Anglican discussions it means Same Sex Marriage? What I have always found fascinating about being a worker priest is how the church behaves as if there is a divide between itself and the rest of the world.'

As an example of a second study of ministry, in November 2011 Dr Michael Clinton of Kings College London carried out his 'Experience of Ministry Survey' (available on line). It was a five year study which seeks to *'inform national strategies for supporting ministry and to shape the future emphasis of continuing ministerial development by asking clergy to share their personal experiences and views'.* Of the two thousand, nine hundred and sixteen responses, almost half were from non stipendiaries. It is interesting to study the whole document, but to pick out a few findings ….... Stipendiaries usually take off one day a week, NSMs are less likely to do so. Dr Clinton's charts showing the time spent on different ministerial activities are remarkably similar for both stipendiaries and NSMs. The survey goes on in 2013 1nd 2015, so watch that space!

174

My personal experience has been that misunderstanding or just plain prejudice about the work of an NSM is quite common within the church (and, interestingly, not so common outside the church!) One tension has been when meeting church-goers who are ossified in a model which has never been exposed to NSM ministry in running or assisting in their parish. In one PCC meeting (not my own parish) I was speaking of being involved in sharing our faith. Someone said 'I didn't join the C of E to be a missionary!' That particular rural PCC was building dominated, resistant to change, deeply suspicious of all hierarchy except their paid priest, inward looking, unwilling to be involved in ministry ('that's what we pay the parson for'), fundamentally ignorant of theological issues, cynical and dismissive, and despite being part of a benefice they always acted in a spirit of competition rather than cooperation. Any wind of change carried an unpleasant wind-chill factor for them, especially when it came to worship style, their preference being for military precision and robotic ritual which outsiders found as warm and personal as an answer-phone. They were God's frozen people, shackled to the past and abdicating responsibility for the future. In the event it turned out that, not surprisingly, they had no future. In-group language and stuffy ritual have little to do with the proclamation of the gospel in the villages and the setting free of those who are bound.

Similarly I have experienced odd treatment from time to time at the hands of paid priests. Once after my incumbent left, the new person took my own parish away from me for some months without any discussion, until local pressure persuaded him to give it back! During an interregnum a trainee curate less than a year from ordination as Deacon tried to take over the whole organisation. That person made some very significant mistakes (earning a bad reputation from offended parishioners) but continued making a mess of things on the grounds that I was 'only an NSM' and as a curate in training they ranked above me! I experienced an archdeacon telling me 'we are not in the business of appointing part-time priests' when a benefice requested that I should work house-for-duty. On another occasion a bishop said he would agree to my leading a benefice ministry team only if I passed his 'test of deployability' (whatever that meant in the context) by moving into a vicarage in a neighbouring parish. At the time I was needing proximity to a motorway junction to carry on my own business serving the Kent constabulary and in any case saw no reason to uproot my family (and my wife's business as a Counsellor) from our own home. He said people would find it easier to know where to find me if I lived in a vicarage: I said they had known how to find me in the benefice for more than a decade to that point, but if it helped I would change the name of our current home to 'the vicarage'.

I failed his test. At that point he made an astonishing (to me) suggestion – that he would give me a stipend to take over a group of churches five miles away and allow me still to live where I was. It was all very bizarre, and anyway my calling was to be a 'tent-maker', to swim with the fishes, so I was not interested. But it wasn't the only time that senior clerics assumed that I might want a 'proper' job as a priest instead of being a 'part-timer'. Big mistake to assume that one day perhaps, once I'd got the hang of the job, I might like to be paid for it!

So even after several decades, NSMs get the impression that mother church is concerned with control and the survival of a system which is self-replicating. They look for ministry candidates who are like the selectors – middle class, safe, conformist. Some selectors would probably be very effective in appointing museum attendants. It could be argued that the C of E will be saved by innovators operating in a range of roles and professions. NSMs often feel that they are not being taken seriously, or you would find us on Bishops Councils and other roles within the organisational

177

structure. There is little theological engagement with our Cinderella ministry. Thinking is ad hoc and varies from diocese to diocese. We are often denied the community of paid ministers in Chapter meetings, training opportunities, conferences and so on. When colleagues operate without reference to us, we will always appear and be made to feel on the periphery of things.

Chapter Twelve

The Final Chapter …..

….. or is it? It is the final chapter for this book, but not for the church. What of the Church of England? Does she have a future? I began the book with dire warnings from various sources that the C of E was on her last legs, but there could be life in her yet. I have tried to adopt Paul's model *'I have become all things to all people, that some may be saved'* – and it works. I recommend NSM ministry as part of the church's answer to some of her current weaknesses. Faith and work must be better integrated in the life of ministry. Being an NSM gives great freedom because everything one does is in a unique way part of building the Kingdom. As I write in the early Summer of 2012, my own Diocese of Canterbury is on a mission called 'Re-imagining Ministry': I think it's a great title because that is what we have to do and the task is huge. The title comes from a book by Revd Dr David Hayward, Director of Pastoral Studies at Ripon College Cuddeston, published by SCM.

I have been sorting through old papers (as one does at retirement) with a view to getting rid of lots of accumulated rubbish after four decades of ordained ministry, and I came across a sermon I wrote forty one years ago in response to a request to address the question 'What is the church for?' I have no knowledge of where my ideas came from then, but in my text I imagined a world in which everyone was tone deaf so that music meant nothing to them. With no delight in harmony, music had become a meaningless noise so that after a few generations people could not enter into the experience that music once conveyed. Musical instruments, having no obvious use, have been abandoned to museums. I questioned whether that could happen to the church. Could the vast majority of people see it as an incomprehensible survivor from the past. Some might value it for pietistic reasons, or as an escape from this complex world, or for archaeological reasons such as its huge buildings with fine architecture. Some might find that the church gives them a sanction to believe that it was founded by a dead clergyman called Jesus who was an early protagonist of the English way of life. But such a church would be a positive hindrance by not taking seriously what God is doing now in his world. God's statement *'Behold I am doing a new thing'* sometimes seems to have been lost.

A non-churchgoer reading reports of church activities might well think that the whole business is a massive irrelevance to their real problems. If the church acts as though God is not concerned with war and peace, hunger and poverty, prejudice, the new possibilities opening through medical and scientific research, and so on, then the church has parted company with the God of history, perpetuating the illusion that God only acted in the past and is only concerned with religious people. Is it possible that after two millennia the Christian institution has become so consumed by irrelevance that it is concealing rather than revealing God to people?

Have we forgotten that the church is what happens when we respond to God's action in the world now? You cannot lock God up inside an institution. It is because God so loved the world that he gave himself for the Roman NCO in the occupying army, for the clerk Matthew working in the tax business, for the fishermen and the old folk, for leaders like Nicodemus and prostitutes, and for each of us. Becoming a Christian is not about going to church, but about becoming a disciple of Jesus. This creates a necessary tension, asking questions about what differences are there between one who is a member of the priesthood of all believers and one who is an ordained priest.

So it is highly relevant to ask the question – 'what is the church for?' I once tried this exercise with my own parish during the Decade of Evangelism, looking for a three to five year development plan which might inform the road towards a new model. I asked the questions one might ask in a business context, about targets, priorities, responsibility for tasks, action plans, resourcing and timetables. We asked 'Where are we now? Where do we want to go? How do we get there? What do I want to get out of church? What are we doing well/badly? What are the factors which facilitate or hinder desirable developments? Is the church spreading faith or just religion?' I can recommend such an exercise at local level from time to time, but I wonder if such brainstorming is ever done at diocesan/national level?

Another useful question is 'What is a priest?' The answer may not be as obvious as we think. It's perhaps easier to say what a priest is not. A priest is not what one writer recently suggested – a man in a dress preaching to grandmothers. A priest is not a pedlar of liturgical mumbo-jumbo, such as the detailed specification of the minutiae of worship. When I was training a kindly old priest spent time with me trying to get me to be an exact copy of himself. It was of fundamental importance to him when presiding at Holy Communion, the precise way in which you held your hands, even specific fingers; when, where and how you turned, knelt, stood, spoke and so on. As far as he was concerned there could only be one attitude to adopt throughout the liturgical performance; to deviate from this strict pattern would lesson the pantomime. One had to enter in total silence, keep that silence for a given count, a courteous greeting to the congregation being anathema. I found however that other churches held equally rigid but quite different displays of liturgical drama. Just how important is this to God or to outsiders? One curate I knew well and tried to work with refused to greet me (or indeed anyone) in the street when she was on her way to give a home Communion, carrying the sanctified elements. People thought she was rude and haughty.

A priest is not a high-priest of tribal initiation rites, 'though it is important to remember at baptisms, funerals and weddings, that God often uses these as means of his grace, despite us. But it is difficult when parents make it quite clear that they have no intention of actually fulfilling their obligations given at a baptism. I once conducted a funeral of someone whose non-believing family told me quite openly that the deceased had no faith at all, and that he was a difficult old git who they were glad to be rid of. Yet they wanted a 'church funeral' It has made me wonder if occasional offices should be formally structured (liturgically) differently for believers and non-believers, or do we just 'keep calm and carry on' in the hope that God does the really important stuff? In passing I must say that it has been my experience that occasional offices have felt much more 'real' when people have approached me from a shared workplace – perhaps it has something to do with a subtle difference between relationship and relatedness.

In the story of the Good Samaritan, it would appear that the priest had a dilemma between what should and what actually does take precedence – the urgent or the important? The story of Chicken Licken shows how easy it is to fixate on silly things from insufficient evidence, as a consequence neglecting the really important. Most priests have felt similar pressure, exacerbated by being the leader of a religious community in which because someone has been paid to do the job, other members never discover their own responsibility for mission. But what exactly should a priest do? Once, in trying to research the role of a priest, I took a Bible and together with a Concordance looked up all the references I could find. It depressed me.

The New Testament was particularly discouraging. It has about one hundred and sixty five references of which about ninety five were in the Gospels. Some were fairly neutral, such as Herod asking the priests where Jesus was to be born, but most seemed to be about priests opposing Jesus, questioning his authority, plotting against him, sending armed soldiers to arrest him, looking for fabricated evidence against him, paying cash for his betrayal, manipulating the mob against him. Jesus meanwhile tells parables against the priests. After Jesus' resurrection the priests continue to suppress his work – putting apostles in jail for instance.

The writer to the Hebrews sees Jesus as the model of a different sort of High Priest which is interesting given that Jesus himself came from a non priestly tribe. I could not find evidence of the early church actually appointing priests in charge of congregations, as we do today. It seems that priesthood was eventually to become a whole new ball game: the old order was defunct and of no use in working out what a priest ought to be doing in the new dispensation.

And the old order? The Old Testament has almost

eight hundred mentions of priests. It appears that priests could also be kings, fathers, allotment holders and even slave owners. They were selected, wore special clothing, anointed, ordained and consecrated, ministered in a holy place. Selected families produced priests in perpetuity but they were chosen from all sorts of people. A priest was allowed to benefit from his work but sometimes it was a matter of luck what he got! They had roles not seen for a long time, such as responsibility to stop the spread of infectious disease, to curse people (especially women it seems!) and to judge people appropriately. Restrictions on their behaviour and relationships extended to their families. Sometimes (so what's new!) priests got drunk, were disgraced, deceitful, murderers, adulterers, profane and showed contempt for God.

Perhaps it is time again to seriously address the role of our priests, whilst allowing the acceptance that of more importance to what priests do, is what they are. It it time for a change? As I remember the priests I have most admired and respected I realise they were rebels in some way. My priestly heroes came from various social backgrounds, training and churchmanship but the thing they held in common was that they were prepared to be innovative for the sake of the Kingdom. They worked out their own particular model for themselves, their church plant and their congregation. They challenged long-held ideas with lateral thinking. They were often unconventional, eccentric, prepared to be fools for Christ.

They worked as if continuing a tradition just because things had always been done that way is a sign of weakness rather than strength. They did not covet the dependence which a child shows for a comfort blanket, knowing that growing up required the faith to change and take risks: maturity is about growing up, not growing older. They knew that change is a sign of life: it is death which has stagnation as its character.

Creatures and institutions which do not evolve become extinct. God's forerunners in the past have met opposition and sometimes a sticky end but in hindsight they have often been viewed differently, positively. Tyndale was burned at the stake for daring to translate the Bible into English at a time when the establishment allowed only graduates to have access to written scriptures, and that in a foreign tongue.

Perhaps we need to find a new balance between Christian work in religion and in the world. Christians have significant and important things to say about God, and the place to say it is in the world. It was Jesus who pointed out that it is the sick who need a doctor, not those who are well. He counselled that new wine needs to go into new wine skins, or disaster will follow. Do NSMs provide an important novel resource to the church in their peculiar role? If so why are they neither treated nor deployed as well as they might be: why do all their dioceses not have a dedicated NSM Officer, or even know what NSMs do? There are about four thousand of us already, so take us more seriously!

But what a dilemma! Many Christians will have had my experience of learning to appreciate the glorious traditions of our church and to love the discipline associated with church practise. But is this a demonstration of our need for religion only, not always connected with Christianity or Jesus' call to bring life in all its fullness into the world? It is so easy to be very busy with the life of the parish church in activities which on reflection are done to preserve the religious status quo – raising money by jumble, fête, market, coffee morning, quiz night, concert, outings, walks – all worthy and enjoyable but not specifically Christian. Of course we have to be attentive to our congregation from Costa Geriatrica (not easy without a loo, which I as a sufferer from prostate cancer know!), but the priest should not be drained by all the visiting and so on. The priest must be aware that (s)he had probably dragged the family kicking and screaming into the same vocation – they need time and attention too.

Oddly, if you can get church people to criticise church, they come up with the same lists – inaudible, clergy person monotone, church too high/low, inadequate music/choir/organist, too cold/uncomfortable/noisy, service hard to follow and not what they are used to – very little mention of anything specifically Christian! Are we, as in the story of Mary and Martha, so busy that we don't take the opportunity to listen to Jesus?

Many denominations such as the Methodists seem to have managed without lots of ordained ministers, local preachers largely running the show whilst they remain at work in the community. This is a reminder that Jesus did not become incarnate to found a society for the preservation of old buildings and old traditions: indeed he insisted that following him meant the need to abandon old ways. He envisaged a church made without hands, composed of living temples made up of faithful followers with Christ as the cornerstone. Too often now 'church' means lovely buildings which are too old, too big, too expensive and with associated management structures.

One of the difficulties which follows from this has its consequence for new Christians who may not see the need for religion as we know it. Often through the lives and testimonies of Christian people outside of the church structure, a person may encounter a profoundly exciting change in themselves which sets them on fire with enthusiasm for Christ. Then perhaps for them, 'church' doesn't just look boring, it feels unnecessary. It does not automatically appear that church is for them.

Jesus was inclusive: all found a welcome except those like the Pharisees with their separatist theology. Publicans and sinners were welcome, those who sought to exclude their neighbour were not. We need to examine our practice to ensure that outsiders (as we wrongly attribute them) do not feel excluded. I am sorry to say that on the whole I have found that doggedly sticking to certain ritual and language can be tremendously excluding to those 'outside'. They find it unnatural, obscure. St Paul warned not to do things which, however good in themselves, would make a brother stumble. Jesus told some that *'you by your tradition have made void the work of God'*.

In this year of anniversary (2012) we are making a deservedly big thing about the importance of the King James Bible, we cannot assume that people will find the use of three hundred year old English somehow more worthy when addressing God and his followers. Any other club which met weekly to converse in Mediaeval English would quite properly be seen as eccentric and out of touch with reality. People would say 'It's OK if you like that sort of thing and I suppose it does no harm, but it's not for me'. I am concerned that when people dismiss what they see as the irrelevance and eccentricities of religion, they might also reject Christianity which is assumed to be the same thing.

It has been my experience that new Christians often find it hard to understand why the church maintains its hierarchy as it does. In a sense, they would be happier with a lowerarchy than a hierarchy! By that I mean that they instinctively understand incarnation to be a downward motion towards people. They read of Jacob's ladder and realise that people are travelling down it, not just climbing upwards. They read about a New Heaven and a New Earth in which God dwells with Man (rather than Man 'going to God' – is that splitting theological hairs?) In his topsy-turvy world, God gets down and dirty, working his way to the bottom.

This makes the organisational structure of the church appear to be quite unlike the servant-hood demonstrated by Jesus. People look at the payroll of the Cathedral, at the dress, language and liturgy of its staff, and ask the question 'Just who is serving who here?' We are spectacularly bad at explaining this. So we need to ask if the current 'management' of the C of E is fit for purpose. If radical change is overdue, what is that change? Does the current set up enhance or inhibit new ways of advancing the faith? Questions, questions, questions .... perhaps we need to formulate some good ones and ask them seriously as we search for our 'fresh expressions'.

Over the next few years stipendiaries are expected to decrease by two hundred year on year. Let us find out how to meet the problems this exacerbates. What is the church for? Why do people go/not go to church?

Such questions recently uncovered interesting answers. In the Lutheran church the answers to why people go to church, in order of importance were: social cohesion; to learn about God; to have fellowship with one another and with Christ; to be forgiven; to hear the word of God; to grow in knowledge of the Bible; to feed the soul; to be loved and encouraged; to be prayed for; to love and encourage fellow Christians; to worship; to promote the gospel. I would love to see a similar poll of C of E members – it might inform on our situation.

In a survey of why people do not go to church, the answers were: too boring or unfulfilling; problems with belief; problems with the moral stance of the church; prefer other forms of spirituality; lack of motivation; bad experiences of church life; lack of time; lack of access (transport, poor health); competing attractions on Sunday; no need to; not a strong belief; the way churches are organised. You may notice that there is little objection to the person and life of Jesus himself!

Are NSMs part of the answer? Despite their increasing numbers, they are largely unknown by the 'man in the street' and ignored by church hierarchy. If you Google NSM you have to persevere or you will learn an awful lot about the Neural Shopping Matrix! The current opinion is that NSMs are not given the encouragement, recognition or support they deserve. Read a diocesan handbook and you will learn negative things: that NSMs are not entitled to fees or rest periods or time off or annual leave and that the diocese has no responsibility for their housing – all pretty negative stuff. Forget the 'one day off each week, 36 days off annually plus Bank and Public Holidays: pro-rata for part-time stipendiaries' because by definition it means zero for those who support themselves financially.

People have to understand that their daily work is of prime interest and importance to God. We spend a huge amount of time at work: if we think that God is not there with us the experience will be useless. People need to be encouraged and taught that their faith has to be lived out in all their life experience. NSMs could be great role models for other Christians at work, but the church as a whole tends to ignore or misunderstand what they do. What they should do is to demonstrate a careful, thought-through model of the values Jesus demonstrated. The church has few programmes to equip people in that way: to enable them to demonstrate Proverbs 3.5-6: *'trust in the Lord with all your heart and don't just trust your own understanding. In EVERYTHING you do acknowledge him and he will make smooth your paths.'*

This is a huge jump for those in church who think that living like Jesus has something to do with living like a vicar rather than a teacher or a hairdresser or a taxi driver. I suggest that Jesus is not particularly interested in religious things, and has no time for the concept of full-time Christian service in the narrow sense. Take God's vocation to work in the conviction that work is of great interest to God! He is interested in everything we do. If 'love one another' is limited to 'church' then I suggest that it is not true that *'by this all will know that you are my disciples'*. John Wesley said: 'The world is my parish' – well said!

Somehow we have equated Christian leadership

with leading a church. The focus needs to shift until every Christian sees themselves as called to lead. The same error is implied by people who use phrases like '(s)he has entered the church' to imply that by becoming 'full-time' (ie. paid!) that person has entered a premier league of Christian service where every other job is secondary and every other Christian is called to finance those who do it 'full-time'. It is my experience that too many churchgoers are allowed to understand that they should support ministry rather than minister themselves. They leave the leadership to those at the pinnacle, as they wrongly see it.

This is not of course new. Decades ago people like Francis Schaeffer said that Christians must influence the seven 'mountains' of society – government, media, arts and entertainment, education, the family and religion, (the last being an interesting choice!) He was passionate that leaders should be called to all those areas to encourage mission and knowledge of the gospel. Yet churches tend to be focussed on themselves, sheltered from the madding crowd, resting from our sinful world, almost totally church-centric. How can we enable believers to become equipped for leadership in their workplace? Is it not the case that the first disciples called (Luke 5) were average working people who in many cases carried on with their day job?

We don't watch from the sidelines – we follow Jesus and in so doing learn how to do what he did, influencing and leading others. Jesus commissioned all to *'go and make disciples'*. Imagine what difference it would make if each church congregation were full of empowered leaders of society, at home and at work, leading as Christ led every day of the week. Jesus presented his work – doing God's will – as the source of his energy, with the extraordinary statement *'my food is to do the will of him who sent me and to finish his work.'* To find out what Jesus is doing and to join in is the only faith that will nourish and sustain. The theme runs through the Bible. Jeremiah said *'Josiah always did right. He gave justice to the poor and was honest. That's what it means to truly know God.'* Amos had a message from God: *'I hate, I despise your religious festivals; your assemblies are a stench to me. Away with the noise of your songs! I will not listen to the music of your harps. But let justice roll on like a river, righteousness like a never ending stream.'* Jesus adds *'I'm telling the solemn truth. Whenever you did one of these things to someone overlooked or ignored, that was me – you did it to me.'* John Stott, commenting on Jesus' 'go and surely I am always with you' says: *'the stay-at-home church will never know the intimacy with God that it so craves, for as Christ taught, it is in the act of going that we encounter his presence.'*

In the end it is always more important and satisfying to follow Jesus than to sign up to institutional Christianity.

I believe that it is time for the church to do what it needs to do every so often – to have a clear-out. It needs to throw out the redundant clutter which gets in the way of a more attractive and relevant Christian lifestyle. It is time to be unsentimental, ruthless. Jesus was quite clear that you cannot put new wine in old bottles. Such a jumble sale would be difficult but we need to be brave. If God is indeed 'The Truth' it is our duty to abandon things which have been shown to be false, whether in doctrine, liturgy, the way we do things, our response to new developments in the world of science, moral questions, whatever. If we insist on continuing with what has been shown to be false, we are being unfaithful to The Truth. The world is rightly very ready to condemn us when we stubbornly refuse to accept demonstrated truth.

Christians are too ready to accept that 'out there in the real world' they will be in great danger, gobbled up by wolves and roaring lions, or have their convictions challenged by people with a different belief. Some believers reside in churches where making challenges, reading 'non-Christian' books, seeing certain films, is assumed to be highly dangerous and destructive to their faith. So they live in a cultural and intellectual ghetto comforted that only they will inherit the kingdom of heaven. But it is 'out there' where Jesus chooses to be ready to meet us, never to leave us. Rubbing shoulders with godless people is something Jesus knows all about. Are we able to face the challenge of new ideas in a world where old certainties about religion can drive people to go into the London Underground with bombs strapped to themselves? We should be very wary of certainties, more open to the God who 'makes all things new'. He is a God who welcomes people who get things wrong, then acknowledge their mistake.

Our faith began simply and was welcomed by people of limited education and none. But over two thousand years it has been cluttered with very sticky debris which hides Jesus from view. Let's scrape it off. We are not here to wallow in the past. Our purpose is not to be spectators but to do things for God who wants to show people his truth. We all have our own part to play in God's drama in the world, but are we prepared to leave our ghetto and step onto God's stage?

I've done the easy bit – anybody can ask questions. But these questions are offered on the back of a long experience of ministry which I would not change, which is in traditional terms unorthodox but is becoming far more common. I offer this perspective in case it triggers useful thought and action. Of course I have been able to give little more than a snapshot of the experience of one NSM – myself. The reader might like to find out if my experience has been typical. There are some excellent resources, usually available for reading online, which give a much fuller picture of the experiences, joys and frustrations of ministers who like myself are non-stipendiary and have been driven to develop ministry outside the confines of a church building. It is not everybody's calling, but it is a majority one, however neglected by the current church.

Printed in Great Britain
by Amazon